Selecting Books for the Elementary School Library Media Center

A COMPLETE GUIDE

Phyllis Van Orden

Neal-Schuman Publishers, Inc.
New York   London

Published by Neal-Schuman Publishers, Inc.
100 Varick Street
New York, NY 10013

Printed and bound in the United States of America.

Library of Congress Cataloging-in-Publication Data
Van Orden, Phyllis.
   Selecting books for the elementary school library media center : a complete guide /
Phyllis Van Orden.
      p.   cm.
   Includes bibliographical references (p.   ).
   ISBN 1-55570-368-2 (alk. paper)
   1. Elementary school libraries—Book selection—United States.   2. Instructional
materials centers—Book selection—United States.   I. Title.

Z675.S3 V36 2000
025.2'1878222—dc21

                                                          99-056349

Contents

List of Tables

List of Color Plates

Preface

Professional book selection requires a broad knowledge of children's literature, knowing one's own biases and how to overcome them, and confidence in making professional decisions. Knowledge gained from working day-to-day with the teachers and learners in a school is the final component needed to build a fine collection.

Selecting Books for the Elementary School Library Media Center focuses on the selection of books in an elementary school and on the resources designed to help someone in that process. Resources that support other aspects of collection development are identified, along with a number of established surveys of children's literature that discuss specific titles.

The school library is the heart of a school. Selecting the books that fill the library's shelves has a major impact on student learning and growth. While *Selecting Books for the Elementary School Library Media Center* provides authoritative guidelines for making quality selection decisions, I firmly believe that each school's library media specialist should decide which titles should be added to that library's collection. This is *not* a responsibility to pass on to an external agency or business.

This book's primary audience is individuals preparing to become elementary school library media specialists and individuals responsible for elementary school library media programs. However, public library children's specialists or librarians in smaller libraries who select children's materials along with managing other areas will find that *Selecting Books for the Elementary School Library Media Center* will help them become effective evaluators of children's books.

Selecting books for elementary school library media collections requires the ability to apply criteria that will evaluate many characteristics of books under consideration, especially: content; literary and artistic elements; physical format; genre; subject; potential use for curriculum, instruction, and recreation; and potential use by individuals or groups. *Selecting Books for the Elementary School Library Media Center* introduces and demonstrates the application of these criteria. It begins with a broad perspective and moves to narrower aspects of selection.

Chapter 1, "Understanding the Selection Process," is an overview of the range of activities involved. Chapter 2, "Establishing and Applying General Selection Criteria," describes criteria that are valid for evaluating all genres. Chapter 3, "Selecting Books That Reflect Our Diverse World," addresses criteria related to multicultural and international aspects of the books.

Chapter 4, "Using Selection Tools," describes the major guides and the reviewing media one can consult in the selection decision process. Once familiar with these resources, the school media specialist will find them to be invaluable aids in selection.

Chapter 5, "Selecting Picture Books," examines the role that illustrations play in picture books. The chapter defines artistic elements, describes factors of composition and choice of medium, and ends with criteria specifically related to illustrations.

Chapters 6 through 10 focus on the special considerations of book selection in specific genres: fiction, genre fiction (mysteries, sports stories, etc.), folklore, rhymes and poetry, and information books. These chapters describe the literary elements of each particular genre and provide a focus for the appropriate criteria.

Chapter 11, "Applying Criteria for Particular Subjects," shows how to apply the appropriate selection standards for biographies, books about the visual arts, how-to-do-it books, and books in science and technology, social sciences, and mathematics.

Chapter 12, "Selecting Reference Books," and Chapter 13, "Selecting Professional Books," provide criteria and list representative titles, authors, and illustrators. In these chapters I have also recommended professional resources for learning more about these particular books.

In all of the chapters, the representative listings are only a starting point on which to begin developing a knowledge of children's literature. Terms in bold are defined in the glossary.

Selecting Books for the Elementary School Library Media Center is designed so one can start with any part of the book that seems interesting; but keep in mind that there is much to be gained from reading the introductory chapters first. After considering the criteria in the first three chapters, I suggest readers skip to a chapter that discusses a type of book with which they are familiar. After reading, for example, the chapter on folk literature, readers could apply the criteria explained in the first three chapters to some familiar folk literature. In the process, they may discover that they already know some of the criteria to consider and will be ready to learn about new ones. Thus they will have started on the lifelong adventure of developing expertise as selectors.

One of the most rewarding responsibilities I have had as a librarian, library educator, and as a member of numerous award juries has been the opportunity to develop my skills for choosing which children's books to add to a collection. It was always an added pleasure to see how selections I had made met the needs of individuals. Seeing a child find joy in a book you have added to the library shelf is one of the greatest rewards librarianship has to offer.

Acknowledgments

The quotations that open each chapter capture for me the spirit of that chapter. In one case, the quotation reminds us of how librarians have a history of commitment to handle their selection responsibilities professionally. That particular quotation, a favorite of mine, is from Helen Haines's *Living with Books* (1950). I also want to recognize one of the tables in the chapter on "Rhymes and Poetry." This table is based on the 1970 writings of Virginia Witucke, and her approach to defining poetry is one that brings clarity to my students.

Colleagues across the country provided testing grounds for the ideas and approaches used in this book. To Virginia for her bountiful ideas, a note of thanks. To Charles and Eileen for their support, a big cheer of hurrah! To Bob, Kay, Pat, Mary, Adele, Sunny, Trudy, and Courtenay, I did try to follow your advice. To John and Cathy, a special note of thanks for expanding my knowledge of the world of art. I hope your enthusiasm passes on to the readers.

Phyllis Van Orden
December 1999

Chapter 1

Understanding the Selection Process

Working collaboratively with teachers and others, the library media specialist is the catalyst for creating collections that promote curricular achievement and information literacy for all learners
— American Association of School Librarians and Association for Educational Communications and Technology, *Information Power: Building Partnerships for Learning*

Selecting books is a satisfying responsibility, one that calls for your knowledge of children: their growth and development, their interests and learning styles, and their literature. Knowledge of the school is also necessary: its philosophy, goals, and program; the needs of the faculty and staff; and the budget. As a school library media specialist, you use this information as you apply criteria to evaluate books and decide which titles to add to the collection.

Selection is a lifelong learning experience. You'll learn about the limitations of your own interests, biases, preferences, blind spots, and, most important, how to put those personal traits aside and make professional decisions. This self-awareness will make you aware of areas in which you will want to seek the opinion of others.

PRESELECTION PROCESS

Before beginning the selection process one needs to know

- the school's philosophy, goals, and curriculum;
- the teachers and their instructional needs;
- the students' interests and developmental, cultural, and learning needs;
- the demographics and other characteristics of the school's community;
- the existing collection;
- the range of quality in children's books.

SELECTION PROCESS

The selection process involves

- applying selection criteria that relate to literary and artistic elements;
- applying selection criteria that relate to each book's intellectual content, organization of information, special features, and physical characteristics;
- applying selection criteria that relate to the unique characteristics of the genre or subdivision the book represents;
- following established policies adopted by the school board;
- comparing a single book to others on the same subject or genre in the collection;
- anticipating who will use a book, how they will use it, and why they might use it.

Selection Procedures

The selection procedure includes:

- consulting and evaluating selection guides and reviewing media;
- knowing how to involve teachers, administrators, and others in the selection process;
- spending within the constraints of the budget;
- following the school's procedures for purchasing and other forms of acquiring books;
- providing full information about the specific title (usually provided on the **verso** [back] of the title page or at the end of the book): author, editor, reteller, compiler; title; series title; edition; place of publication; publisher; date of publication; **ISBN** (International Standard Book Number); and source.

Jobbers and Selection

Jobbers may have print or electronic catalogs that list available titles. Remember, the jobber is selling books to a wide range of libraries; the titles may not meet the needs of your school. Their listings are of what's available—not what's recommended. Even when they list staff as selectors, the catalog is not considered a standard reviewing source. Your use of the reviewing media and the knowledge you gain from your personal examination of new books will guide you as you use the catalogs.

If your school purchases books from a **jobber** (a company that sells books from many publishers), check with other media specialists about the jobber's reputation on order fulfillment, delivery schedule, costs, and replacement policies.

Price of Books

In 1998 over 4,000 titles for young readers were published. During this same time period the average price for hardback books for preschoolers and primary grade children was $15.80; the average price for books for children in grades three to six was $16.03. By 1999 the prices rose to $15.97 for books for preschoolers and primary grade children and $16.27 for books for older children.

Expenditures for Books

It would be interesting to compare what schools spent in 1998, but those figures are not available. Marilyn L. Miller and Marilyn L. Shontz report that during the 1995–1996 school year elementary schools spent an average of $8.49 per pupil and had an average total book budget of $4,272.34 (Miller and Shontz, 1997:32). Satisfying the wide range of needs that any school has with such limited resources requires some very difficult decision making. To make wise decisions one must consider each title carefully.

CRITERIA AND GUIDELINES

Some of the questions you will be asking yourself as you evaluate books are addressed in this book. There are criteria that apply to all books; others apply to specific genres. As you evaluate books you will find that at times some criteria are more important than others for a specific title. Your knowledge of the collection, the needs and interests of the students, and the needs of the teachers can help you weigh the importance of any one criterion.

Information Power *Guidelines*

The American Association of School Librarians (AASL) and the Association of Educational Communications and Technology's (AECT) guidelines for school library media programs *Information Power: Building Partnerships for Learning* identifies specific goals related to the collection. One of the goals is:

> To provide physical access to information through . . . a carefully selected and systematically organized local collection of diverse learning resources that represent a wide range of subjects, levels of difficulty, and formats (AASL/AECT, 1998:7).

The guidelines identify several principles relating to the access of information in the collection. These include that the school library media programs provide "intellectual access to information and ideas for learning" (AASL/AECT, 1998:83) and "physical access to information and resources for learning"(AASL/AECT, 1998:83). These two principles are based on a commitment to the right of intellectual freedom. They also recognize that physical barriers can keep people from intellectual access. For example a partially sighted child will need books with large print formats or books in Braille, while a student using a wheel chair will need wide aisles and low shelves to reach books.

The guidelines also call for the school library media specialist to be "the catalyst for creating collections that promote curricular achievement and information literacy for all learners" (AASL/AECT, 1998:91). Children for whom English is a second language would no doubt enjoy books written in their native tongues, but providing them may seem an impossibility. Locating books for them in English with an appropriate level of vocabulary while meeting their interests also can be a challenge. The unique needs of every child served by the collection, whether the child is a new immigrant, has a physical or mental limitation, or has a preferred learning style, create further demands and call for informed selection decision making. By collaboratively working with teachers and other staff members you can learn about ways that the collection can meet curricular needs and satisfy the students' diverse learning styles.

Genres Guidelines

Genre refers to types of literature sharing common characteristics. Narrative titles such as realistic stories, fantasy, historical fiction, picture storybooks, folklore, and poetry share literary elements. Table 1.1 compares the characteristics of an "effective writer" with a "less effective writer".

As you look at a child's book ask yourself which of the traits below did the author successfully communicate to the reader.

Genres overlap in terms of their characteristics. Literary elements (characters, plot, setting, theme, point of view, style, and tone) function differently in differ-

Table 1.1 Narrative Writers	
Effective writer	**Less Effective Writer**
Well crafted	Poorly written
Characters carefully developed	Characters flat or stereotypical
Conflict developed	Conflict resolved or problem solved in too pat a manner
Character and conflict interrelated	Character does not cause action nor grow from it
Universal theme	Sentimentality or didacticism
Entertains rather than instructs	Tone is didactic, sensational, or sentimental

ent genres. A specific element may be more significant in a particular genre than in others, but the distinction may be blurred. For example, when children seek information the distinction between fiction and nonfiction may be unclear. Many fictional works provide information. Some nonfiction books are a blend of narrative and factual writing. Table 1.2 provides examples of the characteristics of literary elements in various genres.

Award Books as Guides: Newbery Award

One way to see the range of "effective or able writers" is to read some of the Newbery Award and Honor books. The Newbery Award is presented "annually to the author of the most distinguished contribution to American literature for children published in the United States during the preceding year" (Association for Library Service to Children, 1997:3) and administrated by the Association for Library Service to Children (ALSC), a division of the American Library Association. An important factor in this award is the following definition of "distinguished":

- Marked by eminence and distinction: noted for significant achievement
- Marked by excellence in quality
- Marked by conspicuous excellence or eminence
- Individually distinct (Association for Library Service to Children, 1997:3–4)

John Newbery, British publisher in 1744 of the first book designed to amuse children, *A Little Pretty Pocket-Book*. In 1765 he published the first novel written for children, *The Renowned History of Little Goody Two Shoes, Otherwise Called Mrs. Margery Two Shoes.*

					Point of
Genre	**Character**	**Theme**	**Setting**	**Plot**	**View**
Realistic	Characters reflect everyday life	Has a theme	Real and believable	Uses any kind of realistic conflict	Told from a particular point of view
Historical fiction	Act, speak, and have values of time period	Relates to a historical period	Authentic	Focuses on time of stress or change	Told from a particular point of view
Fantasy	Characters believe in their experience/ may not be human	Conveys a universal truth	Imaginary but believable	Uses conflict between good and evil or present and future	Narrator who influences the reader's acceptance of the story
Folklore	Flat and stock characters	Theme of moral with universal appeal	Backdrop	May be between people and animals	No time to go into characters thoughts and feelings
Poetry	Regular or imaginery	Theme of universally understood message			A point of view or a narrator
Biography	Real people	Theme or universal truth	Authentic	Believable problem or goal	Point of view or narrator
Informational	May explain or demonstrate behavior	Central issue or problem	Authentic and provides information		Point of view or narrator

Table 1.2 Characteristics of Literary Elements in Various Genres

Note: Style and tone depend on the author in all genres.

Table 1.3 Newbery Award Books 1990–1999			
Title	**Author**	**Publisher**	**Date of Award/ Publication**
Number the Stars	Lois Lowry	Houghton	1990/1989
Maniac Magee	Jerry Spinelli	Little, Brown	1991/1990
Shiloh	Phyllis Reynolds Naylor	Atheneum	1992/1991
Missing May	Cynthia Rylant	Jackson/Orchard	1993/1992
The Giver	Lois Lowry	Houghton	1994/1993
Walk Two Moons	Sharon Creech	HarperCollins	1995/1994
The Midwife's Apprentice	Karen Cushman	Clarion	1996/1995
The View from Saturday	E.L. Konigsburg	Jean Karl/Atheneum	1997/1996
Out of the Dust	Karen Hesse	Scholastic	1998/1997
Holes	Louis Sachar	Farrar Straus and Giroux	1999/1998

The committee considers

- Interpretation of the theme or concept
- Presentation of information including accuracy, clarity, and organization
- Development of plot
- Delineation of characters
- Delineation of setting
- Appropriateness of style (Association for Library Service to Children, 1999:0 *www.ala.org/alsc/newbery_terms.html*)

The audience for the titles considered by the committee is composed of children up to and including age 14. The announcement is made during the midwinter meeting of the American Library Association, is available at the ALSC Web site at *www.ala.org/alsc,* and is published in the spring issue of *The Journal of Youth Services in Libraries* (JOYS) and in the February issue of *School Library Journal.* Table 1.3 is a list of the Newbery Award books for the past ten years.

The Newbery Award is prestigious. Its prestige raises the question as to whether every school library media program should have a copy of each winner. Yes, if you think the title will add to your collection and be used. No, if you think the title will be of limited use. One reason for taking the "no" position on specific titles is that the books considered for the award are written for people up to and including age fourteen. You may find that some of the plots, character developments, and themes are complex and beyond the comprehension level of the children at your school. If you question the appropriateness of a title, borrow a copy and use it with a few children. You may be surprised at their reaction and their willingness to be challenged even though you may consider the book too mature.

SUMMARY

Being a selector is a gratifying experience that demands that one knows books, people, and the school. The responsibility calls for decision making based on consideration of appropriate criteria. Learning which criteria should have the greatest weight in any given situation is part of this lifelong learning experience. Chapter 2 identifies questions you will use as you make selection decisions.

REFERENCES

[AASL/AECT] American Association of School Librarians and Association for Educational Communications and Technology. 1998. *Information Power: Building Partnerships for Learning.* Chicago: American Library Association; Washington, D.C.: Association for Educational Communications and Technology.

Association for Library Service to Children. 1999. *The Newbery and Caldecott Awards: A Guide to the Medal and Honor Books.* 1999 Edition. Chicago: American Library Association.

Bromley, Karen D'Angelo. 1996. *Webbing with Literature: Creating Story Maps with Children's Books.* 2nd ed. Boston: Allyn and Bacon.

Gerhardt, Lillian N. 1998. "Average Book Prices '98." *School Library Journal* 44, no. 3: 79.

Lukens, Rebecca J. 1999. *A Critical Handbook of Children's Literature.* 6th ed. New York: Longman.

Miller, Marilyn L., and Marilyn L. Shontz. 1997. "Small Change: Expenditures for Resources in School Library Media Centers, FY 1995–96." *School Library Journal* 43, no. 10 (October): 28–37.

Olson, Renee. "Dollar Signs." 1999. *School Library Journal* 45, no. 3 (March): 83.

RECOMMENDED PROFESSIONAL RESOURCES

Children's Book Council. 1996. *Children's Books: Awards & Prizes Includes Prizes and Awards for Young Adult Books.* New York: Children's Books Council.

Describes 213 awards or prizes and the recipients in the United States, Australia, Canada, New Zealand, United Kingdom, and selected international awards

Huck, Charlotte S., Susan Hepler, Janet Hickman, and Barbara Z. Kiefer. 1997. *Children's Literature in the Elementary School*. 6th ed. Madison, Wisc.: Brown & Benchmark.

Provides extensive coverage of the use of children's literature in the school setting along with discussions of genres and individual titles.

Journal of Youth Services in Libraries. American Library Association, 1987— . Continues *Top of the News*. Publication of the Association of Library Service to Children and the Young Adult Library Services Association, two divisions of the American Library Association.

Lukens, Rebecca J. 1999. *A Critical Handbook of Children's Literature*. 6th ed. New York: Longman.

Focuses on literary elements and evaluation of those elements as used by authors in specific works.

Norton, Donna E. 1999. *Through the Eyes of a Child: An Introduction to Children's Literature*. 5th ed. Columbus, Ohio: Merrill.

Integrates discussions of genres, criteria issues, and ways to use books with children. Includes computer disc with database of children's literature titles.

School Library Journal, 1954. Published by R. R. Bowker.

Stein, Barbara L., and Risa W. Brown. 1992. *Running a School Library Media Center: A How-To-Do-It Manual for School and Public Librarians*. New York: Neal-Schuman.

Covers the overall operations of the school library media center and includes a brief section on selection.

Sutherland, Zena. 1997. *Children & Books*. 9th ed. New York: Longman.

Provides extensive discussions of literary genres and individual titles.

Tomlinson, Carl M., and Carol Lynch-Brown. 1997. *Essentials of Children's Literature*. 2nd ed. Boston: Allyn and Bacon.

Identifies milestones in the history of each genre, describes ways to use literature in the classroom, and encourages the use of international literature.

Van Orden, Phyllis J. 1995. *The Collection Program in Schools: Concepts, Practices, and Information Sources*. 2nd ed. Library Science Text Series. Englewood, Colo.: Libraries Unlimited.

Discusses principles of collection development; issues such as intellectual freedom, development of selection, and other policies involved in creating and maintaining a collection; and the use of external resources.

Chapter 2

Establishing and Applying General Selection Criteria

Let the basis of selection be positive, not negative. If the best that can be said for a book is that it will do no harm, there is no valid reason for its selection; every book should be of actual service to somebody, in inspiration or information or recreation.

—Helen E. Haines,
Living with Books:
The Art of Book Selection

Selecting books for a collection involves more than an "I-like-this" action. When purchasing a book for yourself your first question is, Do I like it? or Does it meet my information needs? Your second is, Can I afford it? Selecting a book for a media center collection is more complex. This chapter identifies general guidelines to help you evaluate books. These guidelines, or criteria, serve as an aid in the selection process. There are many reasons for selecting a specific title, and knowing why you select a title is important.

ASKING THE RIGHT QUESTIONS

The first step is to consider the book as communication. Will it be popular? Does it have literary quality? These descriptions may not apply to the same title. Collections need a balance of both. You'll discover what is popular by observing children using books. The questions posed in this chapter will help you develop your ability to judge quality in books.

As you evaluate books, you will be asking yourself questions about each one. Here are some general questions.

- Who could use the book?
- In what ways could they use it?
- Will this book appeal to children?
- What is in the collection? Is this title or a similar work in the collection? Do we need both? Does this title fill a gap in the collection?
- Does this book offer new content or a new approach to the subject?

Selection decisions often are subjective. The purpose of establishing criteria is to guide selection decisions in an objective fashion. Applying the same criteria regularly leads to consistent decision making. You evaluate a book's content, physical form, and potential value to the users. This chapter focuses on general criteria related to the idea of the book (its intellectual content) and the book as a physical item. Later chapters will discuss multicultural aspects, international books, and criteria for specific genres and subjects.

Need for specific information or for a particular type of book may be more important than other criteria. As a selector you will face conflicting needs. One teacher may be very vocal about books she wants to use with her class. Another equally vocal teacher will express a different set of needs. Some children will prefer one type of literature, others another.

Before you purchase any book, remember Helen Haines' advice in the quotation at the beginning of this chapter. What are the strengths of that book? What are its weaknesses? How does it compare to other books?

You want to avoid spending money on a shelf sitter. Here's some practical advice:

- Not all "good" books meet all the criteria.
- One can learn from one's mistakes. Most of us have selected at least a few shelf sitters. Try to figure out what prompted you to buy those books and avoid those actions in the future.
- Read and evaluate as many books as possible so you have points of comparison.
- Observe who uses which titles.
- Read or listen to what others say about a title and see if you agree with them.
- Know the collection so you avoid buying duplicate titles or books with the same information.
- Be prepared to make hard decisions. Trying to meet a wide range of needs when faced with a limited budget is not an easy task.

- Be familiar with the selection policy so you understand the philosophy and other guidelines established by the school and adopted by the school board.
- Have fun as you learn about children's books!
- Do not feel alone in the process. You can ask others to help. You can consult teachers as subject specialists. You can ask teachers about their students' interests and abilities. You can ask children to react to books. In addition to consulting selection guides, seek out opinions of local media specialist colleagues and children's librarians.

INTELLECTUAL CONTENT

What is the idea, the intellectual content, of the book? To judge the intellectual content, you need to apply specific criteria: (1) authority, (2) appropriateness of content to users, (3) scope, (4) accuracy of information, and (5) treatment. You will also be judging the book's organization, literary quality, and special features. All these factors will be weighed along with the number of books available on the subject, the reputation of author or illustrator, and possible uses of the title. Translations and books in series raise more questions for you to consider.

Authority

The term **authority** refers to the qualifications of the people who created the work. Questions to consider:

- What are the author's or illustrator's credentials?
- Has this individual written or illustrated similar works?
- How knowledgeable is this person about this subject or type of literature?

You can look for information about authors and illustrators on the book jackets, in the preface of the book, or in reference works, such as *Something about the Author*. Does the author acknowledge specialists who contributed to or checked information in the book? Is there an "author's note" about the creation of the book or the source of the folktale? You also can look for this type of information in reviews of the book.

Appropriateness

If the content is *appropriate*, the reader should understand the concepts, facts, and fantasies. Questions to consider:

- Is the presentation appropriate for the reader's social and emotional development?

- Is the sense of humor one the reader will understand?
- Will the content be of interest to a child?

No one title will be appropriate for every child. Individual titles may appeal equally well to children at different developmental levels. As you talk with children you will learn which books are appropriate or of interest to each of them.

Scope

Scope refers to the author's goal or the purpose of the book and the breadth and depth of coverage. Questions to consider:

- What is the purpose of the book?
- Does the purpose meet a known need?
- How well does the author fulfill that purpose?
- Does the author state the limitations of the book?
- Does the book present information with an introductory style, in detail, or in a technical manner?

Look for the statement of purpose in the introduction or preface of the book. Examine the table of contents and the index entries to determine the depth of coverage.

Accuracy

Information should be **accurate**. Questions to consider:

- Does the author distinguish opinions from facts?
- Does the author present unbiased opinions?
- Does the author credit the source of photographs?
- Is there an author's note? Does it identify the sources of information used to write the book?
- Is there an acknowledgment section crediting content consultants?
- Is the information up-to-date?

This last question is particularly important for books about science, technology, and political boundaries. Unfortunately, a recent publication date or copyright date does not ensure that this information is correct.

To check the accuracy of information you can compare the information in the book with a variety of sources, including subject-oriented magazines and newspapers. You also can consult with subject specialists (teachers, school personnel, or parents who have an interest in this subject).

Treatment

Treatment refers to how the author presents the material. The style of presentation should be appropriate for the subject and the potential use of the book. Words describing treatment include instructional, authoritative, inadequate, superficial, concise, humorous, emotional, objective, entertaining, moralizing (or didactic), stimulating, or dull. Questions to consider:

- Does the book appeal to and catch the attention of the reader?
- How does the book involve the reader?
- Does the book hold the reader's attention?
- Does the book encourage problem solving by identifying issues or presenting more than one point of view?
- Does the book encourage creativity by suggesting activities?
- Does the book stimulate readers to explore the subject further?
- Does it identify additional sources of information on the subject?
- Does the book deal with concepts the child can understand? If the concepts might be new to the reader, does the text explain them in terms the child will understand?
- Does the author use appropriate vocabulary?
- Does the text explain new terms? If the new terms are explained in a glossary or in footnotes, will this distract the child and compromise the usefulness of the book?
- What role do visual materials (pictures, graphs, and charts) play in presenting the information? Are they an integral part of telling the story or explaining the information? Do they provide visual clarification of the text? Do the visual materials provide information not found in the text? Are the visuals for decorative purposes, adding to the aesthetic appeal of the book, but not providing additional information? Are charts simple and self-explanatory?
- Do the author and illustrator avoid stereotypes dealing with race, sex, and age?
- Does the book reflect our multicultural society?
- Will an adult need to help the child use the book? For safety reasons, children may need an adult to help them use books about science experiments, cookbooks, craft books, and "how-to-do-it" sports books.

EXAMINING THE WORK AS A WHOLE

Organization of Information

Organization affects how easily a reader can locate information. A well-organized text helps the reader move through the information. Common ways of organizing informational books include alphabetically, classification schemes, geographically, chronologically, in tables, or statistically. Questions to consider:

- Does the information flow from one section to another?
- Does the author develop the content logically?
- Can chapters or sections of a book be used independently or must they be read in sequence?
- Does the author emphasize important ideas?
- Is there a summary or review of the major points? (This may occur at the beginning of the book, at the end of each chapter, or in the final chapter.)
- Are different sized types or fonts used to emphasize sections or ideas?

Literary Merit

Literary merit refers to how the author deals with the literary components (theme, plot, setting, characters, and style). The effective author uses these components to create a unity of presentation. One way to test for this unity is to read the book aloud, regardless of the genre. Many nonfiction titles make good "read aloud" books. The significance of each component and the techniques for creating unity of presentation vary from genre to genre. Later chapters will discuss these differences.

Basic questions to ask:

- What is the theme or main idea?
- How does the author present the theme or main idea?
- Is the theme relevant to the child's age, life circumstances, and developmental stage?
- Are the plot, setting, characters, and style consistently organized?
- Does the author catch the reader's interest in the beginning?
- Does the author develop the plot logically?
- Is there a beginning, a middle, and an end to the story?
- Is this a book in which the reader creates the ending, as in interactive stories in which the child chooses from several actions, each of which can lead to a different ending?
- Does the author create plausible, but not predictable, changes and developments?
- Is the description of the time and place clear?
- Are time and place historically, geographically, and politically accurate?
- Are the characters convincing in their actions?
- Is the presentation style or genre appropriate to the theme?
- Does the choice of words and syntax create a mood or convey ideas?
- Does the author use an appropriate point of view (first person, second person, or third person) to tell the story?
- What is your impression of the total effect of the book?

Special Features

Special features (maps; tables; graphs; photographs, and other illustrative materials; glossaries; appendixes; indexes; bibliographies; and recommended reading lists) can be used independently of the main content. Questions to consider:

- Is this information accurately and completely indexed?
- If the information is chronologically arranged, is there a subject index to help the reader locate specific information?
- If the information is alphabetically arranged, are cross-references provided so the reader knows the terms used for the subject?
- Do chapter headings help locate information?
- How does the index help the reader locate information?
- What types of entries are included?
- Given the purpose of the book, will entries for authors, titles, illustrations, illustrators, first line of a poem, or other entries be helpful?
- Are there cross-references in the index? (Test the index by using different terms that mean the same thing.)
- How easy is it to find information in the book?
- Is different sized type used to emphasize selections or illustrations?
- Are the titles in the bibliographies and recommended reading lists for the child, an adult, or both?
- Is the bibliography limited to books, or are other media recommended?
- Is the bibliography annotated?

The value you see in these features can be a decisive factor when faced with a less than clear-cut selection decision.

Reputation of Author and Illustrator

There may be well-known authors and illustrators whose classics you want children to know. Questions to consider:

- Is this a title I want to introduce to children?
- With reissues of classics, is the artwork true to the original?
- Is this title up to the standards I expect from this person?
- Do students and teachers use other works by this individual?
- Will teachers help introduce these works to children?

Award Books as Guides: The Laura Ingalls Wilder Award

There will be other authors and illustrators whose works you feel are important. The winners of the Laura Ingalls Wilder Award include such individuals. The award recognizes authors and illustrators for their substantial and lasting contribution to children's literature published in the United States. The award is an-

Laura Ingalls Wilder
American author, 1867–1957. The first recipient of the award named in her honor is the beloved author of the "Little House" stories, which chronicle her life in the Midwest from 1870 to 1894.

nounced at the midwinter meeting of the American Library Association, is available on the ALSC Website at *www.ala.org/alsc*, and published in the spring issue of *Journal of Youth Services in Libraries* and in the February issue of *School Library Journal*.

Possible Uses

As you evaluate books you will want to think of each one's potential use. Basic questions to ask:

- Who will use this book?
- How will they use it?
- When will they use it?

Other questions to consider:

- Is this a subject of study in the curriculum?
- Is this subject or genre of interest to children?
- Will a student use this book to do a class assignment?
- Could a child use this book for personal information?
- Will a student seek this title for recreational reading?
- Will this book appeal to children who are not skilled readers?
- Could a teacher use this book in an instructional situation?
- Could a teacher use this title for reading aloud?
- Is there more than one audience for this book?

Translations

Words translated into English from another language pose additional questions:

- Is the translation true to the original text?
- Is the translation idiomatic?
- Are the translator's credentials listed?

Table 2.1 Laura Ingalls Wilder Award Recipients	
1954	Laura Ingalls Wilder
1960	Clara Ingram Judson
1965	Ruth Sawyer
1970	E. B. White
1975	Beverly Cleary
1980	Theodor Geisel (Dr. Seuss)
1983	Maurice Sendak
1986	Jean Fritz
1989	Elisabeth George Speare
1992	Marcia Brown
1995	Virginia Hamilton
1998	Russell Freedman

Note: The Association for Library Service to Children administers the Laura Ingalls Wilder Award.

Series

Titles in series often share common characteristics, but you need to judge each book separately. Several authors may write for an information series; not all of the writers may be equally effective.

Questions to consider:

- Does the author of each individual title meet the criteria you use with similar books?
- If one person is author of all the titles in a nonfiction series, is that individual qualified to write on that range of subjects?
- If one person is the author of a series of fiction titles, is that writer able to sustain the reader's interest throughout the series?
- Can the titles be read independently and out of sequence?
- If they are to be read in sequence, is it clear to the reader which title to read first?
- Is this information readily available on the cover, the title page, or the page facing the title page?

Physical Characteristics

The physical characteristics of the book include binding, size, weight, paper, cover, illustrations, and typography. You will judge them independently and collectively. A **trade edition** is a hardback book, such as you find in bookstores. A **prebound book** is one with a reinforced binding put on prior to its being sold. A **paperback edition** is a book with a paper binding. Which do you need? If you anticipate a high number of circulations of a picture book, you may want to consider a prebound or library bound edition. These bindings are sturdier than those found in trade editions. If you want duplicate copies or anticipate that the book will have limited use, paperback editions may be the best investment. If your school sponsors nature field trips, you may want a hardback identification book for the reference collection and a paperback copy to carry on the field trip. Professional reviews and selection tools frequently identify the editions available.

Oversize paperback books, or **big books**, are designed for use with large groups of children reading together. They require storage spaces similar to the bins one sees in poster and print shops. If your teachers use books in this format, evaluate the individual books by considering these questions:

- Does this title have the original artwork and text?
- Do the illustrations help the children read the story?
- Is the shape appropriate for the subject or theme? (A book about trees may be narrow in width and tall in height.)
- How will you store this book?

Books vary in size and weight. You need to think about the children who will use them. Can a young child turn the pages and handle the book with ease? To use one oversize atlas, children quickly learn they need to lay the book on the floor. Naturally this necessitates children lying on the floor as they locate the information they need.

Don't be surprised when children select books because of their size or weight. Some will pick a book they can carry in a pocket. Others will look for the thickest book so they can impress others. In these cases, recognize that the books are not being chosen for content, and indeed they may not be read.

The quality of paper in a book affects its use. Paper so thin that one can see the print from the next page through it is difficult for a new reader to use. Such thin paper also discourages students who are having reading problems.

Use of white spaces, line, and size of type faces (points less than 1/72 of an inch) affect the ease with which a book can be read. *Leading,* the white space between lines, may be as big as the size of the type face (in this example the typical 18 points) for beginning readers. Illustrations, border designs, and color can draw a reader's attention to information. Lines help outline figures, set off charts, and draw attention to a feature.

In *John Jeremy Colton* by Bryan Jeffery Leech, Byron Glaser and Sandra Higashi use different point sizes of 22 fonts to emphasize the flow of the text and to underscore this story about differences. The opening endpapers are in black and white with only one house in green. The closing endpapers show multiple colors in the houses. This reflects the changes that take place in the story. The layout of the text moves around the page, making squiggles and other shapes.

This adds to the aesthetic appeal. However, the reader ends up moving the book around in order to read the text, which is sometimes upside down. Trying to read this book aloud, while showing the illustrations to a group of children isn't easy, but it is fun.

As you consider the book's physical characteristics, here are questions to consider:

- Is the spacing of words and lines suitable for the ability of the students?
- Does white space help the reader see the words?
- Are the size and style of type suitable for the readers?
- Are the illustrations close to the appropriate text? **Note:** Illustrations bound together in one section slow the reading process.

As you observe children using books you will see which formats attract them. Books with moveable parts (toy books, engineered books, and books with transparency overlays) present other challenges. Can the intended reader manipulate the parts? You can anticipate that the parts will become torn after a few circulations. Certainly the reader gets involved with the book. The technique is effective for showing relationships between parts of an object, such as the human body or an automobile.

Aesthetic Quality

Aesthetic qualities can add to the appeal and informative value of a book. Questions to consider:

- Are the illustrations clear and eye-catching?
- Is the packaging attractive?
- Is the book jacket appealing?
- Are colors chosen to express the theme?
- Is there a balance of illustrations to text?
- Is the typeface appropriate for the reader?
- Do the endpapers give a hint of the content?
- Can the viewer see the entire illustration in double-page spreads? (The way the book is bound may eliminate parts of a map or portions of an illustration.)

Availability of Books on the Subject

The lack of other books on the subject can influence a selection decision. An example is the election of a new president. Biographies about that individual may be hard to find. By the end of the president's first term of office more choices will be available. Questions to consider:

- Is there a need for this particular subject?
- Has someone requested this title or a similar one?

Comparison with Other Works

Each book has unique characteristics. As you compare books you will develop the ability to distinguish the elements that make a quality book. To do this, ask yourself these questions:

- How is this book similar to another title by this author or illustrator?
- How is this book different from other titles by this author or illustrator?
- How is this book similar to another title on the same subject or about the same theme?
- How is this book different from another title on the same subject or theme?
- What do reviewers say about this title? Do I agree with their comments? If not, why do I disagree?
- What does the author or illustrator say about this title?
- Do I think this title will have appeal to children over a number of years or will interest in it be for a short time, like a fad?

Cost

Finally, the cost of the book can not be ignored.

- Can I afford the book?
- Is this book a good investment? Does my evaluation of the book indicate that it will be?
- Does the book have enough strengths to justify purchasing it?
- If I cannot afford to buy the book, can I borrow it from other sources?
- Is it one I would recommend when someone wants to make a donation to the collection? (If the answer is yes, start a wish list. People from time to time will ask you for suggestions for memorials and gifts for other occasions, and it is well to be prepared to respond at the moment of interest.)

Books Designed for Beginning Readers

Easy readers, or beginning readers, (books designed for independent use by new readers) often appear in series. They exist in a variety of genres (fiction, fantasy, historical fiction, folklore, poetry, and information books).

Design is a key factor in these works. The books range in length from 31 to 64 pages and are often nine inches by six inches in size. The size of the typeface is larger than that found in books for more experienced readers. The **leading**

Table 2.2 Easy Readers: Characteristics of Levels		
Level One	**Level Two**	**Level Three**
First Grade	Second Grade	Third Grade
17 to 20 point type	18 point type	18 point type
5 words per line	5 words per line	Up to 8 words per line
5 to 7 words per sentence	Slightly more complex sentences alternating with simple ones	Both compound and complex sentences
Sight vocabulary	Increased sight vocabulary	Increased sight vocabulary
One-syllable words of 5 letters or less	Occasional multi-syllabic words	Multisyllabic words
2 to 7 lines per page	4 to 15 lines per page	Up to 15 lines per page
2/3 page used for illustrations and white space	Balance of text with white space and illustration	Text may cover 3/4 of page
		Illustrations may be on alternating pages

(the space between the lines), the wide margins, and the overall use of white space are all designed to help the new reader determine where sentences begin and end. The short text lines consist of one phrase or a very short sentence. Usually there is an illustration on each page.

Some "beginning to read" series titles have controlled vocabularies. One well-known example is Dr. Seuss' *Cat in the Hat* (Random House, 1957), which was based on a limited vocabulary list of approximately 200 easy-to-read words. Another well-known 1957 publication was Else Holmelund Minarik's *Little Bear*, illustrated by Maurice Sendak (HarperCollins).

The primary audience for these series is first through third graders. The characteristics of the three levels are displayed in Table 2.2. A child reading at level three is ready to move into **transitional** books with their greater number of words per line, fewer illustrations, justified right margins, and longer chapters.

SPECIAL CRITERIA

Questions to ask yourself as you evaluate easy readers:

- Does the story begin with short sentences?
- Does the story begin with a simple concept?

- Are the characters introduced within the first two pages?
- Is the setting introduced within the first two pages?
- Is the number of words per line appropriate for the intended reader?
- Is the number of words per sentence appropriate for the intended reader?
- Do new sentences start at the beginning of a line?
- Is there action on every page?
- Is the author able to create appealing repetition?
- Does the author provide a context for new words?
- Will the new words be familiar to the child?
- Is the print large and clear?
- Is space used to separate words and lines?
- Do the illustrations give clues to the text?

Chapter Books

As children develop their reading skills beyond those that are required for the beginning-to-read books, they turn to **chapter books**. They have more words and fewer pictures than the easy-to-read books and are divided into chapters. Ranging from 45 to 100 pages, they have fewer words, a narrower focus, fewer characters, and are less complex than novels for older children. Their audience is the six- to nine-year-olds.

SUMMARY

Although selection decisions can be subjective, through consistently applying objective criteria you will develop your ability to evaluate books. You will evaluate each book's idea, the presentation of the intellectual content, and the packaging of the book. You will consider criteria relating to treatment of multicultural aspects, characteristics of the genre or subject, possible use, intended user, need, and cost. These are the general criteria one uses in evaluating books.

Selection is a complex process. As you make selection decisions and gain a comparative knowledge of children's books, you will find it easier to apply criteria.

TITLES MENTIONED IN THIS CHAPTER

The Cat in the Hat by Dr. Seuss. (Random House, 1957).

John Jeremy Colton by Bryan Jeffery Leech, Byron Glaser, and Sandra Higashi. (Hyperion, 1994).

Little Bear series by Else Homelund Minarik, illustrated by Maurice Sendak. (HarperCollins, 1957).

Something About the Author: Facts and Pictures about Authors and Illustrators of Books for Young People (Gale Research, 1971–).

REFERENCES

England, Claire and Adele M. Fasick. 1987. *ChildView: Evaluating and Reviewing Materials for Children.* Littleton, Colo.: Libraries Unlimited.

Graves, Bonnie. 1998. "First Novels." *Book Links* 7, no. 5 (May): 51–55.

Haines, Helen E. 1950. *Living With Books: The Art of Book Selection.* New York: Columbia University Press.

Harms, Jeanne McLain, and Lucille Lettow. 1996. "Book Design, Part I." *Booklinks* 6, no. 2 (November): 52–54.

———. 1997. "Book Design, Part II." *Booklinks* 6, no. 4 (March): 31–33.

Horning, Kathleen T. 1997. *From Cover to Cover: Evaluating and Reviewing Children's Books.* New York: HarperCollins.

Vidor, Constance. 1994. "Easy-to-Reads: Strategies for Selections." *Book Links* 3, no. 5 (May): 56–59.

RECOMMENDED PROFESSIONAL RESOURCES

Bauer, Marion Dane. 1992. *What's Your Story? A Young Person's Guide to Writing Fiction.* New York: Clarion.

Informative guide on how to write fiction. Although written for children, it includes examples of interest to adults in learning how authors handle characters, plot, point of view, dialogue, endings, and revising.

Christelow, Eileen. 1995. *What Do Authors Do?* New York: Clarion.

Also written for children, this title follows an author and an illustrator from the time they get a creative idea to publication.

Gunning, Thomas G. 1998. *Best Books for Beginning Readers.* Boston: Allyn and Bacon.

Describes the characteristics of and selection guidelines for beginning books. Annotations include bibliographic information, brief sketch of plot, and identification of potential use.

Scieszka, Jon. 1998. "Design Matters." *Horn Book Magazine* 74, no. 2 (March/April 1998): 196–208.

Through text and examples describes the role and the influence of the designer in creating a picture book.

Silvey, Anita, editor. 1995. *Children's Books and Their Creators.* Boston: Houghton Mifflin.

A useful reference about authors, illustrators, genres, and sub-genres that includes brief essays by the creators. The emphasis is on contemporary literature from the United States, but works from other countries are mentioned.

Stevens, Janet. 1995. *From Pictures to Words: A Book about Making a Book.* New York: Holiday.

The author/illustrator creates a story about how she wrote and illustrated a book assisted by imaginative animals that want to appear in the book.

Chapter 3

Selecting Books That Reflect
Our Diverse World

*It is through literature that we most in-
timately enter the hearts and minds and
spirits of other people. And what we
value in this is the* difference *as well as
the human similarities of others.*
—Klaus Flugge, "Crossing the Divide:
Publishing Children's Books in
the European Context"

EXAMINING BOOKS FOR DIVERSITY

As global interaction shrinks our world, the responsibility to help children recognize the similarities and appreciate the differences among people becomes
more crucial. Growing diversity exists in our communities and schools. We work
with children with physical, emotional, or developmental disabilities; from a variety of cultural and ethnic backgrounds; and with native tongues other than English.

Books that portray the similarities and differences include

- books about persons with handicaps/disabilities,
- books about people of diverse cultural and ethnic backgrounds
  (multicultural literature),
- books about countries outside the United States (international literature),
  and

- books translated from their original publication in a language other than English (translations).

SPECIAL CRITERIA FOR LITERATURE ABOUT PEOPLE WITH DISABILITIES

A challenge for any adult working with children is to help the children change stereotypical or negative attitudes. As with the other forms of diversity discussed in this chapter, the goal is to recognize and appreciate the similarities and differences in human beings. A favorite poster clearly states the message: "Label cans, not people". Books portraying people with disabilities can be found in a number of genres including picture storybooks, fiction, and informational works. In fiction the story may be told from the perspective of a brother, sister, friend or by the person with the disability. Photoessay formatted information books can be effective in showing the daily lives of people with disabilities and the types of help they find effective.

As you examine books to address this concern, ask yourself the following questions:

- Are the children presented as unique individuals with the interests, concerns, activities, and behaviors typical of all children?
- Is the person's ability rather than disability stressed?
- Is the accurate description of the disability presented as only one aspect of the person's life?
- Is the emphasis on positive aspects of the person's life?
- Does the character experience the range of achievements and pleasant times that other people do?
- Do the characters solve problems with appropriate help from others?
- Is communication handled in a natural manner?
- Do the characters represent a variety of backgrounds in terms of family, economic level, ethnic groups, and geographical settings?
- Are people with disabilities shown in various roles in society such as workers, community leaders, and participants in social and sports activities?

Professional resources that expand on this topic are listed at the end of this chapter.

SPECIAL CRITERIA FOR MULTICULTURAL LITERATURE

People interpret the term "multicultural literature" in a variety of ways. The Cooperative Children's Book Center (CCBC) of the School of Education at the University of Wisconsin-Madison defines *"multicultural literature* as *books by and*

Buyer Beware
Beware of a book that
focuses primarily on disability,
stereotypes disabled persons as dependent or pitiful, or
uses demeaning descriptions such as "deaf and dumb," "confined to a wheelchair," or "victim of."

about people of color" [italics in original](Kruse, 1992: 30). The Center identifies characteristics of three types of multicultural literature:

1. Being inclusive, broadly presenting the world as one in which all people share common interests and experiences. Multiculturalism is not the main subject of the story. Authors, like Shirley Hughes, are known for presenting an array of individuals.
2. Presenting a multicultural context and written by people of another race or ethnic group. While some people argue that someone who is not from a particular culture cannot adequately portray it, Kruse argues that gifted writers, such as Arnold Adoff, are able to do so.
3. Presenting multicultural content and written by people belonging to the race or ethnic group portrayed. Eloise Greenfield and Laurence Yep are two writers with strong commitments to their heritage. Their themes are universal and of interest to those not represented in the groups they portray.

The collection also should acknowledge the range of subdivisions within a group, such as individual tribes of Native Americans. Books should show individuals in various settings (rural, urban), in different occupations, with different educational backgrounds, in various living conditions, and with varying lifestyles. Within a single book, the same individual may engage in traditional activities wearing traditional clothing and also be seen in contemporary occupations, lifestyles, and clothing.

What should one look for in multicultural books? The Dallas (Texas) Independent School District's selection policy offers the following criteria:

1. Books and other materials should accurately portray the perspectives, attitudes, and feelings of ethnic groups.
2. Fictional works should have strong ethnic characters.
3. Books should describe settings and experiences with which all students can identify and yet accurately reflect ethnic cultures and lifestyles.

4. The protagonists in books with ethnic themes should have ethnic characteristics but should face conflicts and problems that are universal to all cultures and groups.
5. The illustrations in books should be accurate, ethnically sensitive, and technically well done.
6. Ethnic materials should not contain racist concepts, cliches, phrases, or words.
7. Factual materials should be historically accurate.
8. Multiethnic resources and basal textbooks should discuss major events and documents related to ethnic history.

(Dallas Independent School District, Media Services Department. 1993: 4.3.3.3)
Additional questions to consider:

- Are unfamiliar words defined, or can the reader understand them from the context?
- Do minority characters take the initiative in problem solving?
- Are the images of minority characters positive?
- Are racial pride and positive self-image apparent?
- Are descriptions of clothing, hairstyles, food, architecture of home, and customs accurate?
- Does the author's attempt to supply information at a child's level of understanding result in overgeneralization? This may foster inaccuracy and be a form of stereotyping.
- Does the work recognize subgroups of the minority group? For example, does the book recognize that different Native American tribes have particular characteristics and patterns?

The American Association for the Advancement of Science (AAAS) asks reviewers for their publication *Science and Books* to consider AAAS' "Equity Guidelines."

In keeping with our mission of promoting a better understanding of science by the next generation, we feel that it is important to identify materials that are suitable for all audiences and reflective of our diverse, multicultural society.

1. Where appropriate, does the material have equal male/female representation? Is the text gender neutral? In hands-on science books, are girls as well as boys pictured performing the experiments?
2. Are females and minority groups portrayed in a non-stereotypical fashion?
3. Do illustrations, photographs, or film footage include examples of minority group members, senior citizens, or people with disabilities?
4. Would the material be relevant in a wide number of settings (i.e., city,

suburban, and rural) and to a wide spectrum of students (i.e., those who are economically disadvantaged)?

5. In hands-on science books, do the experiments use materials that are accessible to economically disadvantaged students?
6. Would the materials be useful in a multicultural curriculum?
7. Are the materials free of religious bias?
8. Do the materials provide a balanced presentation of controversial (e.g., animal rights) or sensitive (e.g., AIDS) issues? Are dissenting opinions presented fairly? (Gath, 1995: 90)

Reprinted with permission from *Science Books & Films*, vol. 31, no. 3, published by the American Association for the Advancement of Science, 1995.

Professional resources to help you further with the evaluation of books for their treatment of multicultural aspects are listed at the end of this chapter.

Award Books as Guides: The Coretta Scott King Award and The Pura Belpré Award

Since 1970 the Coretta Scott King Award has recognized the efforts of African American authors and illustrators. This American Library Association (ALA) award is administered by the Coretta Scott King Task Force of the Social Responsibilities Round Table. The award recognizes books that promote the culture and contributions to the "American Dream." A source of books on Latino culture is the Pura Belpré Award, presented to Latino writers and illustrators whose work best portrays, affirms, and celebrates the Latino cultural experience in the work of literature for youth. The books, English, Spanish, or bilingual, are selected by a joint committee from the Association for Library Service to Children (an ALA division) and REFORMA (National Association to Promote Library Services to the Spanish Speaking, an ALA affiliate) . The award is presented biennially, and the winners are announced at the ALA Midwinter Meeting, on the ALSC Web site at *www.ala.org/alsc*, and published in the spring issue of *Journal of Youth Services in Libraries*, the February issue of *School Library Journal*, and the February issue of *American Libraries*.

SPECIAL CRITERIA FOR INTERNATIONAL LITERATURE

The increasing number of students for whom English is a second language and the wide range of countries of origin represented by new students serve as reminders of the international basis of diversity in our schools. To help students understand the similarities and differences among these groups, we can turn to **international literature**. Carl M. Tomlinson, editor of *Children's Books from Other Countries* sponsored by the United States Board on Books for Young People, defines international children's literature as that body of books originally published for children in a country other than the United States in a language of that country and later published in this country (Tomlinson, 1998: 4).

Examples can be found in a wide range of genres including books about religion, myths, legends, folklore, poetry, picture storybooks, information, fantasy, and historical fiction. Many classics fall within this category. Representative works include the tales gathered by the Grimm Brothers, *Anno's Journey*, and Anne Frank's *The Diary of a Young Girl*.

Tomlinson further defines these books as including those published in other languages and translated into English, books originally published in English in another country, and books in languages other than English which were subsequently published in that same language in the United States. He excludes "Children's books originally published in the United States for children of this country, but whose characters or settings are foreign" (Tomlinson, 1998: 4).

To ascertain if a book may be considered international, locate information about the place of original publication. This is usually found with the book's cataloging in publication (CIP) information on the verso (back) of the title page or on the last page.

Promoting International Literature: International Board on Books for Young People (IBBY)

A group that actively promotes international understanding and world peace through children's literature is the International Board on Books for Young People (IBBY) founded in 1953. Every two years IBBY sponsors the prestigious Hans Christian Andersen Medal book award. Member countries may nominate a living children's author and illustrator from which an international jury selects the award winners. Five US authors have won the medal: Meindert DeJong (1962), Scott O'Dell (1972), Paula Fox (1978), Virginia Hamilton (1992), and Katherine Paterson in 1998. Maurice Sendak (1970) is the only illustrator from the United States who has won the award.

IBBY's publications include *Bookbird: World of Children's Books*, a quarterly journal of articles and opinion pieces. The International Children's Book Day is observed on or around Hans Christian Andersen's birthday, April 2.

Individuals in the United States can join the United States Board on Books for Young People (USBBY), a section of IBBY. USBBY holds meetings and programs in connection with conferences of the American Library Association, the International Reading Association, and the National Council of Teachers of English. USBBY sponsored the book *Children's Books from Other Countries* edited by Tomlinson. The selection criteria used for including titles in this annotated bibliography can be used in judging books for your collection. Among the criteria they considered were

- high literary and artistic quality (Tomlinson, 1998: 47),
- "worthy and up-to-date treatment of people and their cultures outside the United States" (Tomlinson, 1998: 48), and

- "interesting presentation of information specific to a country other than the United States or presentation of information about the United States from a foreign perspective" (Tomlinson, 1998: 48).

Translations and English-Language Imports

Although no records are kept about translations, it is estimated that less than one percent of the total number of children's books published annually in the United States are translations. The number of books from other countries written in English and then published in the United States is greater. The majority of these English-language titles are from Great Britain, Canada, and Australia.

Both types of books call for careful consideration. Books published in English from other countries may include variants on spelling unfamiliar to children in the United States or use an unfamiliar vocabulary. This can be particularly misleading with information or reference works. When examining such titles, check to see if terms are explained either in the text or in a glossary.

Translations present more complex problems. Clues about the translator may be found in a listing on the title page, the verso of the title page, or on the book jacket. An effective translation is not a simple word-by-word process. The successful translator

- rewrites the original text while maintaining the author's tone, voice, and emotion;
- knows how to make the foreign terms and place names interesting but not confusing to the child reader;
- uses appropriate idioms or substitutes to portray authenticity;
- understands the role of illustration in telling the story.

In summary, Tomlinson notes, "Translators must be skillful writers as well as skillful linguists, and they must be attuned to authors' and readers' sensibilities" (Tomlinson, 1998: 21). Almost always, the translator's native language should be English when the book is being translated into English.

Award Books as Guides: The Mildred L. Batchelder Award

To experience the work of effective translators, try some of the books that received the Mildred L. Batchelder Award. The Association for Library Service to Children administers this award, which is presented to an American publisher

Mildred L. Batchelder
As an American Library Association staff member, Miss Batchelder worked closely with school and children's librarians from 1936 to 1966. She was an advocate for internationalism and for translations of books from other countries.

Table 3.1 Mildred L. Batchelder Award 1990–1999					
Year	Title	Author	Publisher	Translator	Country
1990	*Buster's World*	Bjarne Reuter	Dutton	Anthea Bell	Denmark
1991	*A Hand Full of Stars*	Rafik Schami	Dutton	Rika Lesser	Germany
1992	*The Man from the Other Side*	Uri Orlev	Houghton Mifflin	Hillel Halkin	Israel
1993	No Award				
1994	*The Apprentice*	Pilar Molina Llorente	Farrar Straus and Giroux	Robin Longshaw	Spain
1995	*The Boys from St. Petri*	Bjarne Reuter	Dutton	Anthea Bell	Denmark
1996	*The Lady With the Hat*	Uri Orlev	Houghton Mifflin	Hillel Halkin	Israel
1997	*The Friends*	Kazumi Yumoto	Farrar	Cathy Hirano	Japan
1998	*The Robber and Me*	Josef Hollub	Henry Holt	Elizabeth D. Crawford	Germany
1999	*Thanks to My Mother*	Schoschana Rabinovici	Dial	James Skofield	Israel

of a translated children's book. The award is announced at the midwinter meeting of the American Library Association, is available at the ALSC Web site at *www.ala.org/alsc*, and is published in the spring issue of *The Journal of Youth Services in Libraries* and in the February issue of *School Library Journal*.

The award recognizes the title as being the outstanding translation of a book originally published in a country other than the United States in a language other than English. This award includes books recommended for children up to age fourteen. Some of the titles, such as the 1995 award winner *The Boys from Petri* by Bjarne Reuter (Dutton, 1994), are recommended for middle school students. Others, like Toshi Maruki's *Hiroshima No Pika* (Lothrop, 1982), can be shared with younger children.

SUMMARY

Helping children develop positive attitudes about themselves and about others is an important goal. As you select books for children to help them meet this goal, you need to consider the criteria identified in this chapter about the treatment of people with disabilities, our own multicultural society, and our diverse world.

TITLES MENTIONED IN THIS CHAPTER

Anno's Journey by Anno Mitsumasa. Philomel, 1978.

The Boys from St. Petri by Bjarne Reuter, translated by Anthea Bell. Dutton, 1994.

Diary of a Young Girl by Anne Frank. Doubleday, 1967.

Hiroshima No Pika by Toshi Maruki, translated through Kurita-Bando Literary Agency. Lothrop, Lee & Shepard, 1982.

REFERENCES

Dallas Independent School District, Media Services Department. *Library Media Center Handbook.* 1993. Dallas, Tex.: Dallas Independent School District.

England, Claire, and Adele M. Fasick. 1987. *ChildView: Evaluating and Reviewing Materials for Children.* Littleton, Colo.: Libraries Unlimited.

Flugge, Klaus. 1994. "Crossing the Divide: Publishing Children's Books in the European Context." *Signal* 75 (September): 209–214.

Gath, Tracy. 1995. "Science Books & Films Celebrate 30 Years." *Science Books & Films* 31, no. 3 (April): 65–67, 90.

Kruse, Ginny Moore. 1992. "No Single Season: Multicultural Literature for All Children." *Wilson Library Bulletin* 66, no. 6 (February): 30–34, 122.

Tomlinson, Carl M., ed. 1998. *Children's Books from Other Countries.* Lanham, Md.: Scarecrow. Sponsored by the United States Board on Books for Young People.

Walling, Linda Lucas, and Marilyn H. Karrenbrock. 1993. *Disabilities, Children, and Libraries: Mainstreaming Services in Public Libraries and School Library Media Centers.* Englewood, Colo.: Libraries Unlimited.

Wright, Kieth C., and Judith F. Davie. 1990. *Library Manager's Guide to Hiring and Serving Disabled Persons.* Jefferson, N.C.: McFarland.

RECOMMENDED PROFESSIONAL RESOURCES

Banks, James A. 1994. *Multiethnic Education: Theory and Practice.* 3rd ed. Needham Heights: Allyn & Bacon.
    Introduces reader to terminology, historical background, goals, and philosophical positions, and offers strategies.

Dickman, Floyd. "I Can't Believe It's a Translation." *Book Links* 8, no. 3 (January 1999): 22–26.
    Identifies the criteria used by the Batchelder Committee and describes recent translations.

Helbig, Alethea K., and Agnes Regan Perkins. 1997. *Myths and Hero Tales: A Cross-Cultural Guide to Literature for Children and Young Adults*. Westport: Greenwood.

Marantz, Sylvia S., and Kenneth Marantz. 1994. *Multicultural Picture Books: Art for Understanding Others*. Professional Growth Series. Worthington, Ohio: Linworth.

Describes versions of original tales and folk tales of the past and contemporary times published between 1993 and March 1997 from countries around the world.

MultiCultural Review. GP Subscription Publications, Greenwood Publishing Group, 1992–. Quarterly.

Includes articles, annotated bibliographies, and reviews of materials for children and adults.

Smith, Henrietta M. 1994. *The Coretta Scott King Awards Book: From Vision to Reality*. Chicago: American Library Association.

Provides biographical information about the African American authors and illustrators who won this award and provides sample of their work. The award is announced at the midwinter meeting of the American Library Association, is available on the ALSC Website at *www.ala.org/alsc*, and is published in the February issue of *School Library Journal*.

Tomlinson, Carl M., ed. 1998. *Children's Books from Other Countries*. Lanham, Md: Scarecrow, 1998.

Part One provides background information. Part Two describes how to share international books with children. Part Three is an annotated bibliography of 724 books of all genres from around the world published in English or translated into English. Also provides addresses and Web sites for organizations offering information.

Totten, Herman L., and Risa W. Brown. 1994. *Culturally Diverse Library Collections for Children*. New York: Neal-Schuman.

Guide to 1,300 titles about Native-American, Asian, Hispanic, and African-Americans in biographies, folklore, fiction, nonfiction, and reference books.

United States Board on Books for Young People (USBBY) Secretariat, P.O. Box 8139, Newark, DE 19714–8139 Tel: 302–731–1057, ext. 274 or 229; Fax 302–731–1057 or consult USBBY's Homepage at www/usbby.org

Walling, Linda Lucas, and Marilyn H. Karrenbrock. 1993. *Disabilities, Children, and Libraries: Mainstreaming Services in Public Libraries and School Library Media Centers*. Englewood, Colo.: Libraries Unlimited.

Identifies the types of materials available and how they should be presented for children who are deaf or hard of hearing; blind or with low vision; mobility disabled; cognitively, perceptively, or linguistically disabled; and children with behavioral disorders or learning disabilities.

Zvirin, Stephanie. 1996. "Disabled Kids: Learning, Feeling, and Behaving." *Book Links* 5, no. 5 (May): 15–20.

Addresses how books "can lead children away from harmful stereotypes and labels" (p. 15).

Chapter 4

Using Selection Tools

*Book reviews are essential tools in build-
ing a collection, our link as "solo" librar-
ians to what is being published.*
—Jamie Schomberg, "Tools of the Trade:
School Library Media Specialists,
Reviews, and Collection Development"

Where can you find recommended titles to consider for purchase? Four
commonly used evaluative sources are bibliographies designed to guide
selection, professionally recommended lists, reviewing journals, and bibliographic
essays in professional journals. Reviews reflect the writers' opinions based on their
knowledge of books and experiences with children. The selection guides described
in this chapter are by such knowledgeable and experienced people.

Ideally, selectors prefer to evaluate each book considered for purchase, but
often this is not feasible. There are approximately 5,000 juvenile titles published
each year. Would you have access to all of them. Would you have the time to
personally evaluate each title? These are some of the reasons selectors must rely
on the reviewing media.

EXAMINING SELECTION GUIDES

Each type of selection guide has its advantages and disadvantages. The selected
bibliographies may be comprehensive recommending old and new titles on a wide
range of subjects for children of all ages. Or, they may be limited to be the best
books published in the preceding year. The reviewing journals evaluate recent

publications. Bibliographic essays may evaluate the treatment of a specific topic in old and new titles, compare books within a specific genre, or assess books for specific readers or uses.

If you want to compare these selection guides, identify a recently published child's book with which you are familiar. Then compare your evaluation of it with the comments in the reviews. Do you agree with the reviewer's evaluation? Does the reviewer raise questions about the book or offer new insight you hadn't considered? Reread the book to consider if your assessment will change in view of the reviewer's comments. When you look at the reviewer's qualifications, can you better understand why the perspective is different from yours? Is this a perspective you need to consider?

Selected Bibliographies

Sometimes called "**selection tools**" or "**selection aids**," these bibliographies recommend specific titles. The bibliographies may be extensive works, such as *Children's Catalog* or *Elementary School Library Collection*, or shorter lists, such as the Library of Congress Children's Literature Center annual list *Books for Children*. Typically, for each title they provide bibliographic information, cost, a description, an evaluation, and a recommendation.

Selected bibliographies may

- recommend more than one book on a topic so you can obtain comparative information,
- identify resources for an instructional unit,
- identify books in series,
- recommend titles for reading aloud, or
- identify books for readers at various levels.

Because it takes time for reviewers to evaluate new titles, there is a time gap between the publication date of the last most recent item and the publication date of the selection bibliography itself. Therefore, use reviewing journals for current publications.

You will want to read the introduction to the bibliography to learn about how the selections were made and who was involved in the process. Three common practices for deciding which title to include are 1) recommendations by an individual, 2) recommendations by a committee, or 3) books that received positive reviews in other sources. Also look for the selection criteria used. This important information is frequently not provided, leaving the user in a "buyer beware" position. The introduction to the selection tool should provide clues as to whether a title not included would even have been received in time to be considered.

Special Criteria for Judging Bibliographies

To judge a bibliography, read the introduction, the information about how to use the tool, and sample entries. As you do this, think about the following questions:

1. What is the purpose of the bibliography? Does that purpose meet your need?
2. Does the introduction provide adequate directions for using the bibliography?
3. Does it describe the basis for recommending the titles in the bibliography? Are the criteria stated?
4. Does it explain any symbols or abbreviations used in the entries?
5. Is the bibliography in print, on a CD-ROM, or in other format? Do you have access to the equipment needed to use the bibliography?
6. Who selects the books? Who is responsible for writing the annotations? What are the reviewers' qualifications? Are the reviews signed? Is there a list of the reviewers?
7. What information is provided for each entry?
    a. Check for bibliographic data: full title; authorship (author, editor, reteller); illustrator; translator; series title; place of publication; publisher; date of publication; distributor (if not the publisher); and ISBN (International Standard Book Number).
    b. Check the annotation: Is it descriptive, evaluative or both? Does it recommend the book for specific situations, uses, or audiences? Does it compare this title with other titles? Does the work recommend all titles equally or are there different levels of recommendation?
    c. Do symbols indicate level of recommendation, interest level, readability level, or audience?
    d. What other information about the book is included? This information could be about various editions available, books available in more than one language, or bilingual text.
8. What is the coverage of the bibliography? Does it include only books or all formats used by children? Does it include books for a wide audience or is it limited to books for children? Does it cover all subjects or is it specialized? What periods of publication does it cover?
9. How are the entries organized? Common patterns include a classified scheme such as by Dewey Decimal or classification by broad subjects, audience for the book, author, or title.
10. Does it have indexes to help locate items? Does it provide cross-references? Are there indexes for author, title, series title, audience, reading level, and subject as well as analytics to sections of the books recommended? Are these individual or combined indexes?
11. What is the closing date for the compilation of the bibliography? What is the time gap between compiling the bibliography and its publication?
12. How frequently is the bibliography revised or cumulated? Are supplements provided?

13. Does the bibliography have special features, such as a directory of the publishers of the recommended books, or appendices with additional lists, such as books recommended for beginning readers?
14. What does it cost?

Use these questions as you examine the bibliographies so you can determine their scope, coverage, layout, cost, and limitations and, therefore, how useful they will be to you.

Standard Selection Tools

Two commonly used general selection tools are *Children's Catalog* and *Elementary School Library Collection: A Guide to Books and Other Media, Phases 1–2–3*. A key in using these guides is that all titles listed are recommended—but not equally.

Children's Catalog is published in book format and in CD-ROM format every five years with four annual supplements. *Elementary School Library Collection* is published in book and CD-ROM format every two years. Each of these tools has advantages and limitations. *Children's Catalog* states it is designed to use as an aid in purchasing, user services, verification of information, curriculum support, collection maintenance, and as an instructional aid. (*Children's Catalog*, 1996: ix) *Elementary School Library Collection's* statement reads:

> a primary resource for the continuous development, evaluation, and maintenance of existing collections as well as for the establishment of new library media centers. High quality materials have been selected to meet curricula related needs and personal interests of preschool through sixth grade children. (*Elementary School Library Collection*, 1998: vi.)

A major difference in these tools is their coverage of formats. *Children's Catalog* covers books and magazines for children and some professional library science or children's literature titles. *Elementary School Library Collections* with its curriculum emphasis includes a wider range of formats. These include books for children and professionals working in schools, big books, large type books, periodicals, art prints, study prints, sound filmstrips, sound recording discs, multimedia kits, videocassettes, microcomputer software, videodiscs, and CD-ROM programs.

Children's Catalog is arranged in four sections, first the information books using the Dewey Decimal Classification System regardless of whether the title is a reference work, a professional resource, or a regular nonfiction work for children. Second is the fiction section, followed by short story collections, and ending with easy books for preschool through third grade. The order in *Elementary School Library Collection* is professional collection, reference, periodicals, nonfiction, easy books, and fiction.

The index in *Children's Catalog* provides analytic entries for authors, chap-

Table 4–1 Comparison of *Children's Catalog* and *Elementary School Library Collection*		
Characteristics	**Children's Catalog**	**Elementary School Library Collection**
1. Provides "how to use" directions	Yes	Yes
2. Identifies selection criteria	No	States selection policies and criteria
3. Explains symbols	No	Yes and recommended phase of purchase
4. Identifies format		Yes

5. Provides
  a. bibliographic information: full title, author, illustrator, series title, publisher, date, distributor, ISBN (International Standard Book Number)
  b. Translator
  c. Distributor (if not the publisher)
	Yes
	
	No
	Yes
		Yes
		
		Yes
		Yes

6. Annotations: critically descriptive	Yes	Yes

7. Indicates
  a. interest level,
  b. Readability level
 	
    Bilingual books,
	Yes
	No
	
	Yes
		Yes
		Uses Spache for under third grade, Fry for third grade and up
		Yes

8. Total number of entries	1996 had 6,971 titles; 1997 supplement has 703	In 1996 had 10,790
9. Cataloging information	Uses Abridged Dewey and Sears Subject Headings	Uses Abridged Dewey and Library of Congress Annotated Card Subject Headings for Children's Literature
10. Cost	$105.00	$139.95 or $299.00 with CD-ROM

ters, and subjects within recommended titles. The appendices in *Elementary School Library Collection* provide access with lists of materials for preschoolers, lists for independent readers identified according to the Spache reading list formula for levels 1–1 through 2–2, and a list of author series. Table 4–1 displays other characteristics of these bibliographies.

The price of these tools may seem expensive when your budget is limited. However, consider the many ways people might use these tools. Could teachers use the subject indexes to identify books for specific instructional units? Would the analytical index lead teachers to sections of books that would be helpful in teaching a unit? Will the appendices help you locate titles for children with different reading levels? Can children use the guides to identify resources for projects?

You can use these tools to compare books recommended on the same subject or to check on the availability of a newer edition of a book. These guides can also be used to identify gaps in the collection. You will probably find other users and uses for them. If your media center does not own either of these tools, try to examine them at your school district office or the public library.

Annual Selected Bibliographies

There are two annual publications that include far fewer recommendations, but are less expensive to purchase. As you study Table 4–2 note the difference in coverage from the comprehensive tools discussed earlier. The coverage in these annuals is limited to titles published during the preceding year. *Books for Children* is an annual list of noteworthy books published in the preceding year in the United States. Since 1964, the Children's Literature Center of the Library of Congress has issued this or similar listings for parents, teachers, librarians, and publishers.

Children's Books of the Year is an annual publication by the Child Study Children's Book Committee at Bank Street College, New York. The Bank Street College publication is over 75 years old. A companion publication is *Paperback Books for Children: An Annotated List from the Past and Present Arranged by Age Group and Category*, which provides annotations for 600 titles for preschool through age fourteen. Table 4–2 displays a comparison of these annual bibliographies.

Although both lists cover a wide range of subjects, the limited number of recommended titles hampers their usefulness in identifying books needed to support a school curriculum. In other words, these are highly selected lists recommending a limited number of titles. Such lists and those described in the next section are useful for checking to see if you have overlooked outstanding titles.

Characteristics	**Books for Children** Library of Congress	**Children's Books of the Year** Bank Street College
Table 4–2 Comparison of *Books for Children* (Library of Congress) and *Children's Books of the Year* (Bank Street College)		
Purpose	Recommend "Best of the Year"	Recommend "Best of the Year"
Provides "how-to-use" directions	No	Explains symbols
Lists selection criteria	Yes	Yes
Uses symbols or abbreviations	No	Yes for high interest/low vocabulary, mature readers, outstanding merit
Identifies selectors	Yes	Yes
Provides bibliographic data	Yes	Yes, but does not provide ISBN
Type of annotation:	Descriptive	Critically descriptive
Arrangement	Age of audience	Age and Interest
Includes indexes	None	Author/illustrator, title
Includes appendix and other information	None	Publisher's list, Children's Book Award list, Tips for parents
Number of titles listed	Under 100	Approximately 600
Cost of bibliography	$1.00	$6.00

PROFESSIONAL OR BEST BOOK LISTS

Other sources of inexpensive annual listings include recommended titles selected by members of professional associations. To obtain the lists described here and similar ones, you can contact the issuing professional association or look for the list in the association's publication. Your professional collection may include these journals. If they are not in the collection, you can ask if teachers and other librarians subscribe to them and are willing to share them with you.

As with other bibliographies, you need to read the criteria for selecting titles for inclusion on the list. The label "notable" or "outstanding" title usually indicates a book of quality; however, the title may not meet the particular needs of your collection.

The Association for Library Service to Children's annual "Notable Children's Books" list uses the term notable as including "books of especially commendable quality, books that exhibit venturesome levels (through age 14) that reflect and encourage children's interest in exemplary ways." Usually the list includes sixty-some titles including all genres. The list is available online at *www.ala.org/ alsc/nbook* and is published in *Booklist*, usually the April issue, and in the March issue of *School Library Journal*.

The National Science Teachers Association's annual "Outstanding Science Trade Books for Children" appears in the March issue of *Science and Children* and is available online at *www.nsta.org/pubs/sc/ostblist.htm*. The committee considers a book's accuracy, its readability, and the compatibility of the text, format, and illustrations for the intended audience, pre-kindergartners to eighth graders. The subjects included are animals, archaeology, anthropology, paleontology, biography, botany, chemistry, mineralogy, environment, conservation, geology, meteorology, human body, sexuality, nature, life, ocean and shore life, physics, technology, and engineering.

A parallel list, "Notable Children's Trade Books" by the National Council for the Social Studies, appears annually in the April/May issue of *Social Education*. Criteria for inclusion is that the books:

1. are written primarily for children in grades K-8,
2. emphasize human relations,
3. represent a diversity of groups and are sensitive to a broad range of cultural experiences,
4. present an original theme or a fresh slant on a traditional topic,
5. are easily readable and of high literary quality, and
6. have a pleasing format and, when appropriate, illustrations that enrich the text. (*Notable Children's Trade Books*, 1997:2).

Recommended titles include works of fiction, poetry, folklore, and information. These are arranged by the thematic strands of the social studies curriculum: culture; time, continuity, and change; people, places, and environments; individual development and identity; individuals, groups, and institutions; power, authority, and governance; production, distribution, and consumption; science, technology, and society; global connections; and civic ideals and practices.

JOURNALS WITH REVIEWS

Journals with their reviews of current titles provide the major source of information that aids selection decisions. They may cover a broad range of subjects or focus on one subject. Examples of subject-oriented journals are *Appraisal: Science Books for Young People* and *Science Books & Films*, which will be discussed in the chapter on information books.

Each reviewing journal has unique features. These unique characteristics create advantages and limitations for the user. The journals may

- be produced by different types of publishers (commercial firms, professional associations, or education agencies),
- be aimed at specific audiences, such as media personnel or classroom teachers,
- focus on one format, such as books, or cover a wide range of formats,
- focus on materials for potential users—children in kindergarten through sixth grade, preschoolers through adult, or
- focus on a particular perspective, such as the consciousness-raising efforts of *Multicultural Review*.

Four commonly used reviewing journals, *Booklist: Includes Reference Books Bulletin, Bulletin of the Center for Children's Books, Horn Book Magazine,* and *School Library Journal*, illustrate the different approaches. *Bulletin of the Center for Children's Books* clearly explains the symbols used for its recommendations, including titles not recommended. The *Bulletin* is one of the few journals that prints reviews for titles not recommended. *The Horn Book Guide*, a semiannual companion to *Horn Book Magazine*, includes reviews for titles not recommended and provides ratings of recommendations for titles whether listed or not in *Horn Book Magazine*, which only reviews recommended titles. The reviews in *School Library Journal* are by school library media specialists, children's librarians, and library educators. *Booklist* includes reviews of books for preschoolers through adults. You will learn the importance of using more than one reviewing journal, as no single journal provides all the information you need to make selection decisions.

Examine the journals to become familiar with their purpose, coverage, and selection process. You also will learn to pick up clues about the background of reviewers, who may be journal staff members with a wide range of experience with children's books or professionals working with children. Look for signed reviews or a list of reviewers with information about each person's position and background. Once when I purchased three books that were "shelf sitters," I searched past reviews and discovered that all had been highly recommended by the same person. After that experience I became cautious about buying books recommended by that individual. It was obvious that she worked with children whose interests and abilities were different from those with whom I worked.

What do media specialists look for in reviews? The list includes:

- Descriptive reviews with objective statements about plot, characters, theme, and illustrations.
- Evaluative statements including comparison of the title with similar books.
- Identification of potential appeal, curriculum use, and possible controversial aspects.

Problems media specialists face in relying on the reviewing journals include:

- Time lag between publication and review. Check the journal's policy about how close to a book's publication date they will do a review. Conversely, after what period of time will they not do a review? If the journal uses reviewers working with children there may be a delay due to the shipping and handling of the book. The advantage to this is that children's reactions may be noted in the review.
- Lack of access to reviewing journals for specific subjects. For example, reviews about mathematics and science books receive greater coverage in subject-oriented reviewing journals than in the commonly used broad-based journals.
- Lack of reviews in more than one journal for specific titles. The number of issues per year varies from journal to journal, as does the number of titles reviewed each year. Study the journal's policy to identify limitations on what or when they review.
- Uneven quality or relevance of reviews. Even if you are able to locate the reviews, the assessments can vary in quality or applicability to your collection. Note the position and geographical location of the reviewer to decide if his or her situation could be similar to your own.

Because reviews can vary in quality or applicability to your collection, you will find the practice of comparing two or more reviews useful in making your decision. Cumulated indexes in the journals can be valuable in the search for reviews. Table 4–3 compares some characteristics of commonly used reviewing journals.

BIBLIOGRAPHIC ESSAYS

Bibliographic essays describing books on a particular subject, theme, use, or for a specific audience are another source of recommendations found in journals. These frequently appear in *School Library Journal* and in *Book Links*. The essays can be very helpful, but they demand careful reading. An omitted item may not be recommended, but the reader does not know whether the writer simply overlooked the item or does not recommend it. Bibliographic essays usually focus on a specific component of an item and often do not provide an overall assessment of each title mentioned in the essay.

		Bulletin of the Center for Children's Books	Horn Book Magazines	School Library Journal
Features	**Booklist**			
Frequency	*Bi-weekly*	*Monthly*	*Bi-Monthly*	*Monthly*
Publisher	American Library Association	Graduate School of Library and Information Science, University of Illinois	The Horn Book, Inc.	Cahners
Age targeted in reviewed materials	Preschool through adult	Three year olds to ninth graders	Infancy through young adult	Preschool through young adult
Formats reviewed	Books and other formats	Books	Books	Books, Films, Videos, Recordings, CD-ROMS, Computer Software, Professional books
Index for each issue?	Yes	Yes	Yes	Yes
Index for year?	Semi-annual; August and February 15	Annual, July/August issue	Annual, November/ December issue	Annual, December
Selectors	Staff	Staff	Staff	School Library Media Specialists, Children and Young Adult Librarians
Other coverage			Articles	Articles
Cost	$65.00	$35.00	$42.00	$79.50

Table title: **Table 4–3 Comparison of Commonly Used Reviewing Journals**

SUMMARY

School library media specialists rarely have an opportunity to personally evaluate the thousands of children's books that are published annually. They consult selection sources, including bibliographies, professionally recommended lists, reviewing journals, and bibliographic essays. Knowing that reviews are expressions of the reviewer's opinion, media specialists can compare their own assessment of a specific book with those of reviewers. This process helps to evaluate the reviewing tool and at the same time may provide an opportunity to learn to examine books in new ways.

TITLES MENTIONED IN THIS CHAPTER

Appraisal: Science Books for Young People. Boston University School of Education, Children's Science Book Review Committee, Department of Science and Mathematics, 1967–

Book Links: Connecting Books, Libraries, and Classrooms. American Library Association, bimonthly.

Booklist: Includes Reference Books Bulletin. American Library Association, 1905–

Books for Children, 1964—. Washington, DC: Library of Congress, 1994. Order from U.S. Government Printing Office, Superintendent of Documents, Washington, DC 20402–9329; $1.00 prepaid.

Bulletin of the Center for Children's Books. Graduate School of Library and Information Science, University of Illnois, 1945–

Children's Books of the Year 1998 Edition: Books Published in 1997 by the Child Study Children's Book Committee. Annual. New York: Child Study Children's Book Committee at Bank Street College, 1998. Order from Bank Street College, Child Study Children's Book Committee, C35, 610 W. 112 St., New York, NY 10025; $8.00 plus $2.00 for postage and handling prepaid check to Child Study Children's Book Committee or contact the Committee at 212–875–4540; *bookcom@bnkst.edu*; *www.bnkst.edu/bookcommittee/booklist.html*.

Children's Catalog. 17th ed. H. W. Wilson, 1996. Includes four supplements. 0–8242–0893–5.

Elementary School Library Collection: A Guide to Books and Other Media, Phases 1–2–3. 21st revised ed. Brodart, 1998. 0–87272–119–1.

The Horn Book Guide to Children's and Young Adult Books. Horn Book, 1990–

The Horn Book Magazine. Horn Book. 1924–

"Notable Children's Books" by Notable Children's Book Committee of the Association for Library Service to Children (ALSC), a division of the American Library Association. The list is available from the ALSC office, ALSC Notable Books, 50 E. Huron St., Chicago, IL 60611 (Include a stamped self-addressed #10 envelope); and is published in the March issue of *School Library Journal*.

"Notable Children's Trade Books" by a Book Review Committee of the National

Council for the Social Studies in cooperation with the Children's Book Council. The list is published in the April/May issue of *Social Education.*

"Outstanding Science Trade Books for Children" is a cooperative effort of the Children's Book Council and the National Science Teachers Association. The list is published in the March issue of *Science and Children.*

Paperback Books for Children: An Annotated List from the Past and Present Arranged by Age Group and Category. (Bank Street College address given above, $6.00 prepaid.)

School Library Journal. R. R. Bowker, 1954–

Science Books and Films. American Association for the Advancement of Science, 1975–

REFERENCES

Bishop, Kay, and Phyllis Van Orden. "Reviewing Children's Books: A Content Analysis." *The Library Quarterly* 68, no. 2 (April 1998): 145–182.

Children's Catalog. H. W. Wilson, 1996.

Elementary School Library Collection: A Guide to Books and Other Media, Phases 1–2–3. Brodart, 1998.

"Notable Children's Books: Function Statement." Chicago, Ill.: Association for Library Service to Children, nd.

"Notable Children's Trade Books, April/May 1997." *Social Education* 50, no. 4, Pull-Out Section (April/May 1997):2–16.

Schomberg, Jamie. 1993. "Tools of the Trade: School Library Media Specialists, Reviews, and Collection Development." In *Evaluating Children's Books: A Critical Look: Aesthetic, Social, and Political Aspects of Analyzing and Using Children's Books,* ed. by Betsy Hearne and Roger Sutton, 37–57. Allerton Park Institute, no. 43. Urbana-Champaign, Ill.: University of Illinois, Graduate School of Library and Information Science.

RECOMMENDED PROFESSIONAL RESOURCE

Horning, Kathleen T. *Evaluating and Reviewing Children's Books.* New York: HarperCollins, 1997.
Provides background about the different genres with examples of specific titles, identifies terms used in creating such books, and describes how to create a written assessment.

Chapter 5

Selecting Picture Books

> We perceive new experiences in terms of
> the experiences preceding them. . . . each
> picture in a picture book establishes a
> context for the picture that follows—[it]
> becomes a schema that determines how
> we will perceive the next picture.
>
> —Perry Nodelman,
> *Words about Pictures:*
> *The Narrative Art of*
> *Children's Picture Books*

EXAMINING PICTURE BOOKS

When one hears the term **picture book**, one often thinks first of the genre in which pictures and text play equally important roles in the narrative. These types of picture storybooks will be discussed in another chapter. Picture book also refers to books with a specific format. Usually 32 pages in length, these books may be 48 or 64 pages long. The pictures alone may tell the story as in the case of wordless books, such as David Wiesner's *Tuesday*. Or, a combination of words and pictures may give the information as in biographical works, such as Jean Fritz' *And Then What Happened, Paul Revere?* illustrated by Margot Tomes.

There is a wide variety of books in which pictures convey the story or information. Examples include alphabet books (*Alphabet Tale* by Jan Garten, illustrated by Muriel Batherman); counting books (*Big Fat Hen* by Keith Baker); concept books (*Color Zoo* by Lois Ehlert); folk literature (*Beware the Brindlebeast* by Anita Riggio); myths and legends (*The Robber Baby: Stories from the Greek Myths* by Anne Rockwell); historical fiction (*Pink and Say* by Patricia Polacco); information books (*Hello! Good-bye!* by Aliki); modern realistic fiction (*Smoky Night* by Eve Bunting, illustrated by David Diaz); and poetry (*Street Music* by Arnold Adoff, illustrated by Karen Barbour).

Audience range for the picture book format is wide. Picture books are **crossover books**: a marketing term for books of interests to both young readers and adults. For example, *Publishers Weekly* reports that Jon Scieszka and Lane Smith's *The True Story of the Three Little Pigs* sells well to the 18- to 30-year old crowd (Maughan, 1995: 24), not just to children.

The content of a picture book may be a simple story. For example, in *Good Night Gorilla* by Peggy Rathmann, pictures and a minimum number of words describe how a gorilla leads the animals to the zookeeper's home. The content of a story may be less obvious in a work like *Time Flies* by Eric Rohmann. This wordless book can be viewed at several levels. The reader who has prior knowledge of the debate about the relationship between dinosaurs and birds brings a greater appreciation to the experience than one who does not. Yet both readers can enjoy the book. Another complex example is David Macaulay's *Black and White*, which tells four related stories simultaneously on each double-page spread.

A picture book differs from an **illustrated book** in which occasional illustrations serve a decorative purpose rather than extending the text. In some works of fiction each chapter is introduced by an illustration. Another example is found in anthologies, where an illustration may indicate the subject of each section.

Barbara Elleman, former editor of *Book Links*, argues that

> we need to give time and attention to children's aesthetic growth and to looking quietly and thoughtfully at well executed art. . . . The artwork available in children's books is wide-ranging in style, technique, and media, and offers a natural opportunity for introducing children to art (Elleman, 1994: 5).

As you examine the pictorial elements, composition, media, book design, and styles found in children's books, you will appreciate her observation about the wide range of artwork available to children.

Because illustrations play a major role in communicating the message in picture books the quality of these illustrations is of the utmost importance. To evaluate picture books you have to use your knowledge and appreciation of the techniques of illustration and book design. One way to improve your skill is to consult books about art. Two useful titles are *Looking at Pictures: An Introduction to Art for Young People* by Joy Richardson and *The Painter's Eye: Learning to Look at Contemporary American Art* by Jan Greenberg and Sandra Jordan.

Randolph Caldecott was a 19th century English illustrator known for the action in his illustrations, the vitality of the drawings, and the display of humor. The Caldecott Medal bears reproductions of his illustrations of John Gilpin's ride in William Cowper's poem "The Diverting History of John Gilpin" and "four-and-twenty blackbirds baked in a pie" from the Mother Goose nursery rhyme "Sing a Song of Sixpence."

AWARD BOOKS AS GUIDES: CALDECOTT AWARD

You also can examine the Caldecott Award and Honor books for examples of excellence in picture books. This award honors the illustrator of the most distinguished picture book for children published in the United States during the preceding year. The Association for Library Service to Children, a division of the American Library Association, administers the medal. The award is announced at a press conference during the midwinter meeting of the American Library Association, is listed on the ALSC Web site at *www.ala.org/alsc*, and is published in the spring issue of *The Journal of Youth Services in Libraries* and in the February issue of *School Library Journal*.

The purpose of the award is to encourage original and creative works in the field of books for children up to age 14. The artist must be a citizen or resident of the United States. The committee may select additional distinguished books as Honor books.

Distinguished is defined as:

- Marked by eminence and distinction; noted for significant achievement
- Marked by excellence in quality
- Marked by conspicuous excellence or eminence
- Individually distinct (Association for Library Service to Children, 1999: 00; *www.ala.org/alsc/caldecott_terms.html*)

Dorothy P. Lathrop received the first Caldecott Medal in 1938 for *Animals of the Bible*, text selected by Helen Dean Fish from the King James Bible (Lippincott, 1937).

Books to help you with artistic terms and provide various visual approaches are listed at the end of this chapter under the heading Recommended Professional Resources. Both children and adults can use some of the recommended resources.

PLATE 1

Illustration from *Grandfather's Journey* by Allen Say. Copyright © 1993 by Allen Say. Reprinted by permission of Houghton Mifflin Company. All rights reserved.

Medium: Gouache paints

The use of grays close in value provides a background setting for the weight of the three characters, which form one shape balanced by the white (lack of color) crisp lines of the ship's railing. The horizontal lines of the decking repeated in the shapes in the background show this is a docked boat.

PLATE 2

Illustration by Donald Crews from his *Freight Train.* Copyright © 1978 by Donald Crews. By permission of Greenwillow Books, a division of William Morrow and Company, Inc.

Medium: Paint applied with an air brush

Shape, space, edge, and color are used to create motion and balance. The color of one car flowing to the color of the following car and the blurred lines of the wheels create motion. The asymmetrical placement of the train suggests its motion onto the next page. The soft edge of the airbrush is in contrast with the linear drawing of the trestles.

PLATE 3

Illustration from *Hosni the Dreamer: An Arabian Tale* by Ehud Ben-Ezer, pictures by Uri Shulevitz. Text copyright © 1997 by Ehud Ben-Ezer. Illustration copyright © 1997 by Uri Shulevitz. Reprinted by permission of Farrar, Straus & Giroux, Inc.

Medium: Watercolors

Shape, space, line, color, and detail create exaggeration, perspective, and rhythm. Authentic desert colors establish the setting. The rhythm of people moving fills the space and captures the busyness of the market place. Although the buildings are exaggerated, care is given to details such as the Arabic writings on the buildings and architectural ornaments. Strong use of line defines shapes and creates patterns combined with watercolor shadows to bring a three-dimensional quality to the illustration.

PLATE 4

From *John Henry* by Julius Lester, illustrated by Jerry Pinkney. Copyright © 1994 by Jerry Pinkney, illustrations. Used by permission of Dial Books for Young Readers, a division of Penguin Putnam, Inc.

Medium: Pencil, colored pencil, and watercolor

John Henry dominates this scene in terms of his size, position of his body, and his placement on the page. Line, light, color, and shadow give volume and movement creating a three-dimensional appearance adding depth to the illustration, while focusing the viewer's attention on John Henry. John Henry's body's asymmetrical position is balanced by the darker colors of the boss's clothing and the steam drill.

PLATE 5

Illustration from *Honest Abe* by Edith Kunhardt. Illustrations by Malcah Zeldis. Copyright © 1993 by Malcah Zeldis. By permission of Greenwillow Books, a division of William Morrow and Company, Inc.

Medium: Gouache paints

This folk artist uses intense colors and exaggerated sizes for Douglas and Lincoln to suggest their power as speakers. In using flat, two-dimensional figures with details reflecting the historical period and setting, Zeldis focuses on Lincoln's grandeur and importance, making Lincoln appear larger than life. Smaller figures function as a decorative element in the illustration.

Finally, when his daughter was nearly grown, he could wait no more.
He took his family and returned to his homeland.

Plate 1

Crossing trestles.

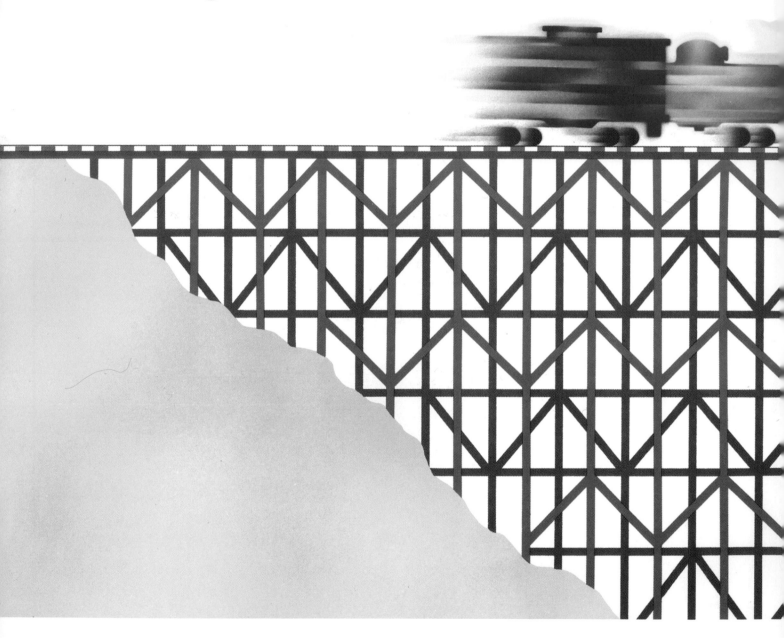

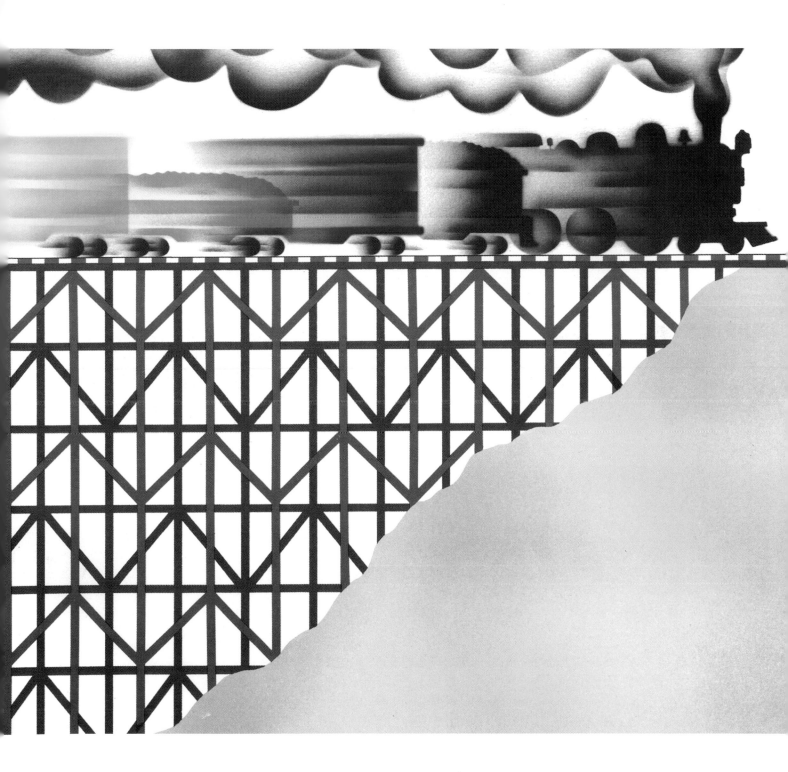

Plate 2

After crossing a large wadi—a riverbed that was dry—they
finally reached the city.

The sheikh sold his camels. He paid each shepherd a gold
dinar and gave them the rest of the day off to enjoy the wonders
of the city.

The shepherds hurried off together, leaving Hosni on his
own.

Hosni wandered through the city's streets, amid the noisy crowd. The more he walked, the more the city felt like his dream, and like the tribal elders' tales. Only now it was real, and even more exciting than he had imagined.

He went to the city's market, passing by the shops and stands with their colorful cloth, embroidered robes, carpets, shiny pots and plates. The scent of pilaf, kebab, falafel, couscous, and sweet halvah filled the air. But Hosni didn't buy anything.

Plate 3

Plate 4

A few years later Abe decided to run for the United States Senate. He ran against Stephen A. Douglas. Douglas believed that slavery should continue. Lincoln believed that slavery should end. Lincoln and Douglas traveled all over Illinois, debating each other. When the people voted, Douglas won, but the debates made Lincoln famous.

Plate 5

The world will little note, nor long remember what we say here, but it can never forget what they did here.

Plate 6

Thereafter, Kchokeen could foretell the giant waves that marked Gonakadet's travels at the mouth of the bay. The trembling of the earth and the sound of the sea told her much, but it was the howl of the bear that meant a wave was coming. The fishermen were grateful for her predictions, because now they could travel the waters in safety. The village prospered, and the people accorded Kchokeen great honor and wealth.

Plate 7

Plate 8

I am a cat
and I arch my back.
Can you do it?

I can do it!

Plate 9

plate 16

Plate 10

PLATE 6

Illustration from *The Gettysburg Address*. Illustration copyright © 1995 by Michael McCurdy. Reprinted by permission of Houghton Mifflin Company. All rights reserved.

Medium: Scratchboard

Line and detail with contrasts and perspective create a realistic scene. The black-and-white illustrations depict the somber tone of the Civil War. In this particular scene the carefully detailed features of the audience help the viewer focus on Lincoln. The inclusion of their reactions to his famous words provides a vehicle for involving the viewer in the event. The mood of the illustration mirrors the impact of the text.

PLATE 7

Illustration from *The Wave of The Sea-Wolf*. Illustration copyright © 1994 by David Wisniewski. Reprinted by permission of Houghton Mifflin Company. All rights reserved.

Medium: Cut paper

Layers of intricate shapes, exaggerated waves, and high contrast of the brightness and jaggedness of the white paper against the blue sky draw the viewer's attention to the background wave that forewarns of coming events. Wisniewski layers intricate shapes upon each other to build a diorama filled with excitement and action.

PLATE 8

Illustration from *Tuesday*. Illustration copyright © 1991 by David Wiesner. Reprinted by permission of Clarion Books/Houghton Mifflin Company. All rights reserved.

Medium: Watercolors

The realistic detail of setting, emphasized by perspective, muted colors, and moonlight shadows makes the impossible believable. The placement of some of the frogs moving off the page leads the viewer on to the next scene.

PLATE 9

Copyright © 1997 by Eric Carle. Used by permission of HarperCollins Publishers.

Title: *From Head to Toe* by Eric Carle (HarperCollins, 1997).

Medium: Collage

Large white spaces contrast with the bold, clear colors. The blue and black of the cat directs the viewer's eye to the child's hat. The position of the eyes and body stances unite the two sides of this double page spread.

PLATE 10

Illustration from *Smoky Night* by Eve Bunting, illustrations copyright © 1994 by David Diaz, reproduced by permission of Harcourt, Inc.

Medium: Collage, acrylics, linocut

Heavy black lines set off the illustration from the border and outline the figures. The large curving shape of the woman is balanced by the vertical stance of the boy and cat. The extended arms of the woman and the elongated shape of the cat direct our focus to the dish of milk. Yellow is a dominant and hopeful color at this turning point in the story.

| | | | | Date of Award/ | |
Title	Illustrator	Author	Publisher	Publication	Medium
Lon Po Po	Ed Young		Philomel	1990/1989	Watercolor, Pastels
Black and White	David Macaulay		Houghton	1991/1990	Watercolor, Ink, Gouache
Tuesday	David Wiesner		Clarion	1992/1991	Watercolor
Mirette on the High Wire	Emily Arnold McCully		Putnam	1993/1992	Watercolor
Grandfather's Journey	Allen Say		Houghton Mifflin	1994/1993	Watercolor
Smoky Night	David Diaz	Eve Bunting	Harcourt	1995/1994	Acrylic, Mixed-media collage
Officer Buckle and Gloria	Peggy Rathmann		Putnam	1996/1995	Watercolor, Ink
Golem	David Wisniewski		Clarion	1997/1996	Papercuts
Rapunzel	Paul O. Zelinsky		Dutton	1998/1997	Oils
Snowflake Bentley	Mary Azarian	Jacqueline Briggs Martin	Houghton Mifflin	1999/1998	Woodcuts

Table 5–1 Caldecott Award Books, 1990–1999

UNDERSTANDING THE ELEMENTS OF PICTURE BOOKS

How do you examine picture books? One technique is to look at the book several times. Each time concentrate on a different aspect. What clues do the cover and book jacket give you about the content and purpose of the book? Next look for clues on the endpapers inside each cover. Does the color of the paper or the illustrations suggest the book's content? Can you find clues on the title page and its facing page? Even the illustrations on the dedication page can add to your anticipation of the book's content. Read the book attentively. Concentrate on both the illustrations and the text. Ask yourself, "How does the overall presentation of the literary and pictorial elements of the book tell the story?"

Then reread the book and concentrate on the illustrations. Questions to consider:

- How do the pictures tell the story? Or present the information?
- Do they convey meaning and emotion?

- Do they show the relationship of shapes?
- What do they tell you about the setting of the story?
- If there were no text, could you tell the story?
- How are colors used in the book?
- Are the illustrations limited to the primary colors (red, blue, and yellow)?
- Are the colors bright or pale, soft or harsh, cool or warm?
- Can you determine the medium the artist used?
- What overall impression do you have of the uniqueness of this book?

Next concentrate on details in the illustrations. Do any of the details reappear in the various illustrations? In books designed to motivate the young child, look for details that will involve the child. *Have You Seen My Duckling?* by Nancy Tafuri is an example of a book in which the text and illustrations invite the child to look for the missing duckling.

As you use picture books you and the children can answer the following questions: What information do the details provide? Do they reflect a historical period or a culture?

Evaluate the pictures as art. What techniques did the artist use? How do these techniques create a mood, provide information, focus the reader's attention on the action of the story, reveal the setting, or show changes in the characters? And finally, do you think the qualities of the book will bring enjoyment to a child?

Pictorial Elements

Artists, regardless of their style or choice of medium, decide how they are going to effectively use the **pictorial elements** of shape, line, space, edge, color, proportion, and detail to tell the story. One can equate the pictorial elements with an artist's vocabulary; these elements serve the same purposes as words and syntax for authors.

The artist can use lines, colors, and value to create **shapes** or to outline some mass. Shapes can be recognizable objects, animals, or people; they may be geometric or abstract. The shapes may be flat and two-dimensional or fully rounded, giving a three-dimensional impression. Shapes can suggest rather than portray objects. Look for shapes that suggest feeling and ideas. The shape of an object may give the viewer a sense of its perspective. The viewer may sense the dimensions and volume of the object. You will find many effective examples of the use of line and shapes.

Eric Carle, well known for his collages, uses shape, space, and color to create contrast, motion, and unity in *From Head to Toe* (plate 9). The call for physical exercise is delivered with an upbeat approach. The large black letter text and large areas of white space contrast with the clear colors of the figures. The double-page illustration's use of facing shapes communicates how to do the exercise. The paint strokes suggest motion and textures. The blue and black of the cat directs the viewer's eye to the hat of the child. The position of the eyes and body stances unite the two sides of the illustration.

An artist creates a **line** with dots that can go in any direction. It may be a straight line, a sharp one, an angular one, or one that curves. The line can be broken. It can be thick or thin, dark or pale. Lines may be soft, fluid, following contours, or they can be quickly drawn; both can create movement. Lines can define an object and give substance, shape, and mass. All this can be done in black and white.

Lines vary in their angle, width, length, motion, and color. Each use helps the artist communicate in a different way. Lines can visualize the character's actions, interactions with others, inner thoughts, and feelings. Often lines are used to outline a shape or form or to imply depth and texture.

In *Smoky Night* (plate 10) by Eve Bunting, David Diaz uses shape, line, color, and proportions and creates balance, emphasis, and focus. Yellow is used throughout this story of the Watts riot. In this illustration the protagonist's cat has been found after the fire and yellow—the color of the sun and suggestive of new beginnings—is used as a dominant and hopeful color. Heavy black lines set off the illustration from the border and outline the figures. The large curving shape of the woman is balanced by the vertical stance of the boy and cat. The extended arms of the woman and the elongated shape of the cat direct our focus to the dish of milk. This event plays a role in moving the story forward, foreshadowing the book's climax. A unique feature of this book is the collage used as background for the text and illustrations. Photographs of harsh, heavy, and sharp objects capture the chaos of a riot.

Artists use **space** in illustrations to create negative areas (empty) or positive areas (enclosed). The artist's use of these two types of spaces can create balance in the illustration. Whether dealing with an abstract or realistic painting, artists use the same techniques to create perspective or the illusion of depth. They may use overlapping planes, converging lines, color, scale, size, and placement to create a two-dimensional or three-dimensional effect. For example, paler and less intense colors may be used to create a faraway effect. Colors in the background may be softer and blur. In the two-dimensional illustration the object or figure remains distinct. In the three-dimensional illustration the objects or figures might overlap. The artist thus focuses our attention by creating a point of view in the space.

In *Hosni the Dreamer* (plate 3), Uri Shulevitz uses shape, space, line, color, and detail to create exaggeration, perspective, and rhythm. A shepherd travels across the desert to the city to spend his fortune. Using the authentic desert colors of the region, Shulevitz enlivens the text with his charming drawings. This is a good example of the importance of the integration of text and illustrations in a picture storybook. Here the illustrations play a key role in establishing the setting and the mood of the story. Shulevitz fills the space with the rhythm of people moving to capture busyness of the market place. While exaggerating the shape of buildings, he pays attention to details such as the Arabic writings on the buildings and the architectural ornaments. His strong use of line to define shapes creates patterns, and with his use of watercolor shadows he brings a three-dimensional quality to the illustration.

Other artists use **edge**, rather than a line, to create shape. To create the edge, the artist may use a contrasting color to distinguish the shape from the background or another object. When an artist makes a collage, different materials create the edge.

Picture books can be in color or in black and white. Variations in black and white illustrations can be created by adding black to mix shades or by adding white to mix tints.

When using **color** the artist is involved with its three attributes: hue, intensity, and value. **Hue** refers to the six pure colors: red, orange, yellow, green, blue, and violet. You probably can find color wheels in some of the reference materials in your collection. For an example of how artists use the primary colors of red, yellow, and blue with other colors see Joy Richardson's *Looking at Pictures*. Colors with red in them are considered warm, while colors with blue in them are cool. The artist's choice of color thus affects the mood of the picture.

Intensity refers to the brightness or dullness (the strength) of a color, which can be made duller by adding the color opposite it on the color wheel. For example, adding blue makes orange duller.

Value refers to the lightness or darkness of a color and can be changed by adding white or black. Artists also use shape, line, and texture to create value contrasts. Changing the value with color or shadings of black and white helps create space, identify characters, suggest a change in time, create mood, reflect action, and give a sense of setting.

In *Grandfather's Journey* (plate 1), Allen Say uses shape space, line, color, value, and detail with balance and repetition. The muted soft watercolors capture the mood of this story of remembrance. In these realistic, almost portrait-like, drawings viewers feel like they are looking at a family photo album. The positioning of the bodies and the details of facial expressions reveal a dignified and reflective spirit. The weight of the three characters as one shape are balanced by the white (lack of color) crisp lines of the ship's railing. The horizontal lines of the decking repeated in the background shapes show that this is a docked boat. The use of grays close in value provides a background setting without distracting from the emphasis on the family. The contrast of the hazy details and faded background further add reality to the setting.

Proportions, the relationship of the size of one object with another, may be realistic or highly exaggerated. Dr. Seuss's use of exaggerated proportions adds to the humor of his stories. In contrast, realistic proportions are more desirable in a concept book dealing with relationships of objects. (**Concept book** is a term used to describe the category of books in which basic information is presented, usually for the young child.)

The amount of **detail** used by the artist also influences the message being delivered. Many objects can be complex or create a very busy illustration. This approach can effectively present an activity involving many people or reflect a character's state of mind. Fewer details provide a simpler style, one desirable in helping very young children focus on a particular object.

Michael McCurdy in *Gettysburg Address* by Abraham Lincoln (plate 6) uses line and detail with contrasts and perspective to create a realistic scene. The black and white illustrations depict the somber tone of the Civil War through detailed and accurate drawings of the battle scenes and war maneuvers. The struggle of the people is rendered so realistically that it brings new energy to this historical era. Using fine lines and high contrast, McCurdy emphasizes ethnic and gender diversity as well as action in his realistic portraits. In this particular scene, the detailed features of the audience watching Lincoln point the viewer's attention to McCurdy's focal point, Lincoln on the stage. The inclusion of their reactions to his famous words provides a vehicle for involving the viewer in the event. The mood of the illustration mirrors the impact of the text.

Contrast this illustration with that by Malcah Zeldis (plate 5).

A folk artist, Malcah Zeldis in *Honest Abe* (plate 5) by Edith Kunhardt uses intense colors and exaggerated sizes of Douglas and Lincoln to suggest their power as speakers. The naïve style and the typical intense use of colors by this folk artist highlight the presence of Abraham Lincoln in each of her paintings. In using flat two-dimensional figures with details reflecting the historical period and setting, Zeldis focuses on Lincoln's grandeur and importance, making him larger than life. Notice how effectively the exaggerated size of Douglas and Lincoln suggests their power in contrast to the sizes of the audience figures, which reflect their lesser role in history. Here these smaller figures function as a decorative element in the illustration.

Composition

Artists also make decisions about how they are going to organize the elements. This involves unity, balance, rhythm, perspective, and proximity. Writers arrange words to provide a message; artists arrange pictorial elements to create a message. The artist aims to achieve a sense of unity within the illustration. **Unity** is the result of the artist's technique in relating various parts of an illustration to each other to create an integrated whole. To determine whether this was achieved Jan Greenberg and Sandra Jordan assert that

> when you look at a unified work of art, you feel it. If you were to remove one line or shape or color, the painting might fall apart. If you were to add another part, it would be too much (Greenberg and Jordan, 1994: 68).

The artist rearranges the elements in the composition to achieve unity.

In *Tuesday*, David Wiesner (plate 8) uses color and detail to create perspective, rhythm, and unity. Flying frogs travel over a city in a nighttime adventure. In this fantasy voyage Wiesner uses his humorous paintings to give the reader a bird's eye view of the frogs' adventure in flight. Looking down upon the houses we see the realistic detail of setting, emphasized by perspective, muted colors and moonlight shadows making the impossible believable. The reoccurring image of frogs on each page reinforces the central theme of the book and unifies the story. The placement of some of the frogs moving off the page leads the viewer on to the next scene.

Balance is one of the important aspects of composition. Balance may be symmetrical or asymmetrical. If the parts of the illustration are arranged so the shapes, patterns, and colors are identical on either side of a central boundary, then the work is **symmetrical**. When the halves are not identical, the work is **asymmetrical**. Color, lines, shapes, and sizes are used to create the balance. A smaller shape of a bright color may attract more attention than a larger space of a dull color on the page.

In *John Henry* (plate 4) Jerry Pinkney uses line, color, proportion, detail, asymmetrical placement, and perspective. In this retelling by Julius Lester of a legendary African American hero, John Henry's forward leaning position presents a statement of his eagerness to face this new challenge. This stance portrays not only his eagerness but also his strength. John Henry dominates this scene in terms of size, body position, and placement on the page. His body is in an asymmetrical position. Line, light, color, and the use of shadow give volume and movement, creating a three-dimensional appearance that adds depth to the illustration while focusing the viewer's attention. The choice of lighter and brighter colors for John Henry enables the viewer to notice more detail in his features and clothing than for the other people in the illustration. The darker colors and lack of contrasts limit the impact of the boss's clothing and steam drill and provide a balance for John Henry.

The **rhythm** in the illustration expresses movement by repeating colors, shapes, lines, or texture. This sense of motion in the picture causes the eye to move from one part to another. The artist may use techniques such as repetition of patterns or lines to create this effect.

In *Freight Train*, Donald Crews (plate 2) uses shapes, space, edge, and color to create motion and balance. The influence of graphic art is evident in this book about colors. The color of each car flows into the color of the following car. Motion is also seen in the blurred lines from the wheels. The airbrush technique creates a sense of motion; the soft edge of the airbrush contrasts with the linear drawing of the trestles. The asymmetrical placement of the train suggests its motion onto the next page and is contrasted with the flatness of the rest of the illustration. The large size text on white space balances the black of the engine and the smoke, while the bottom half of the illustration is balanced by the soft yellowish-green background.

Variety in textures, lines, colors, and shapes provides contrasts and visual interest. All of these in turn can direct the viewer's eye to the movement and help us see from the artist's viewpoint.

The artist uses lines and patterns to lead the viewer's eye to what the viewer is supposed to see (**perspective**), whether it be motion, activity, stability, or calm. One way the artist might do this is to use a character's arm or an arrow to direct the viewer's attention to a specific place in the painting.

There are other ways the artist engages the eye or evokes feelings. **Proximity** refers to the location of various objects in relationship to each other. The artist may choose one dominant object or a visual element to catch the eye. For example, one character or object may be placed closer to the viewer and thus appear larger than the other characters or objects. The artist may accent or highlight certain features by exaggerating them. The artist may choose to use objects similar to or very different from each other.

David Wisniewski, noted for his cut paper illustrations, uses shapes, color, detail, contrast, and exaggeration to help the reader focus in his *Wave of the Sea-Wolf* (plate 7). An Indian princess is rescued from drowning and saves her people. An original story based on Northwest Indian lore inspires the dramatic cut paper illustrations. Wisniewski layers intricate shapes upon each other to build to a diorama filled with excitement and action. In this scene the figures of Tlingit people, wearing customary clothing, point the viewer to the distant mountain. The exaggerated waves forewarn of coming events. The high contrast of the brightness and jaggedness of the white paper against the blue sky draws the viewer's attention from the more evenly colored foreground to the background wave. All the figures cast a shadow upon the background, making this a three-dimensional drama. A border of tradition Northwest Indian motifs continues the theme by framing the text.

Medium

Artists employ various media—each with unique qualities—to create distinct effects. You will find a wide range in picture books. Information about the medium used may be provided in the book, usually on the **verso** (back) of the title page, in the blurb on the inside of the book jacket, or in a biographical sketch about the illustrator on the back flap of the book jacket.

The original artwork may be drawn using pencils, pen and ink, pastels, watercolor, or paints. Other illustrations are the result of printmaking in which woodblock prints, engravings, or silkscreen are used. And still other illustrations may be photographs. Artists may use a combination of materials and create collages.

The artist might do a preliminary sketch using pencils and then use them for the final illustrations. A graphite pencil is used to create lines: hard pencil to create a thin line, a soft one to create a heavy line. An array of neutral tones can be achieved using only black and white. Mixed colored pencils can create various hues. Other tools used in drawings that can create lines, shadings, and shadows include pen and ink, markers, crayons, and chalk.

Pastels, a soft chalky drawing material similar to charcoal, are available in a wide range of colors. The artist can create a slightly textured, flaky surface by pressing heavily with the pastel or create a softer effect by blending the colors. When the artist uses a light touch the results are sketchy marks and less intense colors.

Watercolor, a powder color mixed with water, can be used on watercolor paper, which is usually white. With the transparency of the watercolors, the paper creates the light areas. Artists may use ink lines on the watercolors to define forms.

Gouache (opaque watercolors), made by mixing water directly into a powdered pigment, is opaque and hides what is under it. This can create intense color, as the amount of pigment prevents the reflection of light. **Tempera** is formed by mixing colored pigment with a binder and water; it dries quickly and permanently, so it is harder to achieve subtle colors with it. **Poster paint** is a form of tempera.

Acrylic paint is water soluble until it dries and then becomes water-resistant. It can be applied with a brush or palette knife to achieve different effects.

Mixing color pigments into an oil base makes **oil paints**. As the oil dries slowly the artist can mix colors or remove mistakes. Different degrees of thickness result in different textures.

In **printmaking** the drawn item is reversed when printed. The artist chooses from a variety of materials to transfer one image to another. In an early method, one seen less frequently today, the artist cut into a wood block, removing pieces, and creating a raised surface (in relief). When inked, this surface pressed against the paper creates a reversed impression of the design or image as a **woodblock print**. The artist may do a similar process using a **linoleum block** creating a linocut. **Etching** is a process in which the drawings are reproduced from a metal plate on which acid has been used to create the lines. Another common form of printmaking is **silk screening**. In this process the artist creates a stencil by blocking out parts of the silk. The ink is squeezed through the open mesh of the silk on the paper. The image is not reversed as in the other forms of printmaking.

Scratchboard gives the appearance of a woodcut. This is created by the artist's scratching a picture into the surface of a two-layer board. The result is a high contrast between the remaining and scratched away areas.

Some illustrations are comprised of multiple materials, including fragments of colored papers, photographs, fabrics, or pieces of wood. These materials are then glued to a flat surface creating a single picture. To create a three-dimensional effect the artist may use objects, such as safety pins, or embossing.

Photographers using black-and-white or color film create other illustrations. As an artist, the photographer uses techniques of framing, composing, and printing pictures. As the painter presents a viewpoint, so does the photographer. Tana Hoban effectively uses the camera to make small objects large or the distant close in her concept books.

Graphic artists can also use technology. David Pelletier's *The Graphic Alphabet* is an example of the use of computer-generated images reproduced in full color. Seymour Simon's *The Heart: Our Circulatory System* uses images from x-rays and photographs that were scanned and computer coded to create clear, colorful illustrations.

Sculptured media can be created using plastine, which is then photographed. This form of modeling clay never gets hard, so the artist can reshape the piece.

Design

The appearance and appeal of a picture book reflect the work of the book designer. These individuals make decisions about the shape, size, binding, endpapers, paper, typefaces, and page layout.

The shape of a picture book is usually a rectangle. In some cases the height of the rectangle exceeds the width. An example of this is *A Tree is Nice* by Janice May Udry (also available in Spanish, *Un Arbol Es Hermos*). The shape of this book reflects the subject of the book. Other books may be wide, allowing the illustrators to create larger pictures using facing pages. *Time Flies* by Eric Rohmann provides an example of the artist using the two-page spread to give a sense of movement and size of the objects. While the shape of a book can give a hint of its content, the variety of shapes also makes these books the most difficult to shelve. They often require deeper shelves than many libraries have. Dividers in shelves can help keep these books straight, whether they are picture storybooks or information books.

The **front matter**, or the pages between the front endpapers and the first page of text, may also be illustrated. Illustrations may appear on the half-title page, the frontispiece, the title page, and the dedication page. Here one may find clues to the mood, characters, setting, theme, or subject of the book. In *Ginger Jumps* by Lisa Campbell Ernst, the cover, the endpapers, and even the page with the copyright and cataloging-in-publication information provide the setting of the story. The copyright notice and cataloging notes are in the form of a rose-colored poster advertising the circus. the "Commendably Concise Collection Convenient Congressional Cataloging" headline is printed on a bannerlike scrolled ribbon. The humor and color indicate the story's light hearted, but earnest, mood.

Patricia Polacco's dedication page in *Pink and Say* is a good example of how authors and illustrators use illustrations on this page. Polacco uses a double page spread portraying a black family seeing the eldest son off to the Civil War. The text, "To the memory of Pinkus Aylee," introduces the reader to this black Union soldier who saved the life of a white Union soldier.

Page shape can vary from the book shape. You will find half pages, where the top might contain one story and the bottom another, or the top page can be used with various bottom pages, or a variation of the above. The technique of trimming pages so each one is bigger than the page before can help direct the reader's attention to the movement of the story or a change in size or detail. Other techniques include die-cutting a part of the page so the reader sees something from the following page or using a clear transparent page with information about the illustration under it.

Sizes range from very small, such as Beatrix Potter's books, to very large ones like *Time Flies*. The larger size permits sharing with a group of children.

Binding refers to how the book is encased. The designer is interested in creating an appealing book with a durable exterior. Sometimes an illustration appears on the cover, other times a design motif.

Book jackets, protective covers for the book, also provide information about a book. They prepare the users for what will come. The illustration used may be the one that is on the cover, one from the book, or a separate work. When the illustration extends over both sides, you have a **double page spread**. Sometimes the book jacket has two illustrations: the front one giving a hint of the content, the back reflecting the end of the story. Information provided on the inside of book jackets includes biographical information about the author and illustrator and a description of the contents.

Endpapers are the first and last spreads inside the front and back cover. The endpapers may be plain or introduce a motif used throughout the book. Pictures used on the endpapers may forecast the content, provide information, or create the mood for a story. Characters may be introduced. The colors of the endpapers may feature colors used throughout the book, suggesting the mood of a story.

The choice of paper can add to the sensory experience of handling a book. The paper may have a matte finish (a dull surface) or be coated with a shiny surface. The paper should not dominate or weaken the artwork. For young readers or those having difficulty reading, avoid thin pages in which the text from one page can be seen on the reverse page.

Typefaces used in the text (text faces) also affect the look of the book. For beginning readers the selection of text faces can facilitate access to the information or make it easy to read. These may differ from the display faces used on the title page or for chapter headings. The size of the text face (measured in points) also affects the appearance and accessibility of the book. As you examine books, look to see if the typeface is aesthetically pleasing with the illustrations.

Typefaces used on title pages and for the chapter headings are called **display faces**. They are usually larger and more decorative than the text faces.

Introduce children to typography with Carolyn Falwell's *Letter Jesters*, where you will find colorful illustrations and definitions for terms such as roman/italic, light/bold, *serif/sans serif*, plus information about the effect typestyle creates. Children may want to word process different fonts and different sizes to see the effect.

Page layout refers to where the type and illustrations are placed on the page. In some books a frame or border sets off the text or pictures. In other books the text may be above, below, to the right, to the left, or in a combination of locations in relation to the pictures. The text can also be on the illustration. As you look at the book, ask yourself if the child will be able to follow the flow of words or if the busyness of the page is confusing.

The term double spread refers to two facing pages. An illustrator may do one painting using the two pages, which gives the artist the advantage of having more space and room in which to illustrate. The place where the two pages come together is called the **gutter**. In a carefully prepared book the picture (created by the artwork on each of two pages) matches. Illustrations in the gutter create a problem when one is thinking about having a book rebound and there is no room for the necessary trimming.

So far we have looked at the characteristics of the traditional book format of flat two-dimensional pages. Today there are many books that involve construction details used by book designers and paper engineers. Within this category are pop-up books, lift the flap, pull the tab, revolving wheels, sliding panels, and toy books. The interactive characteristics of these books attract users. Some of the information books help children see the relationships of parts of an object or person. The big drawback for libraries is the limited number of times these books can circulate without needing replacement. A part pulled completely out of the book cannot be replaced easily.

Other books contain moveable parts, such as game pieces, materials for science or handicraft activities, and audiocassettes in the book or attached to the cover. The first user enjoys the book; the second may not be able to use the book if a part is missing. If you work with preschoolers, pay attention to warning labels on some board books with parts potentially harmful to children.

SPECIAL CRITERIA FOR PICTURE BOOKS

The following questions are designed to help you examine picture books. No one book will or should have all the qualities mentioned. They are options to look for in the illustrations and there is no one right answer. You will need to judge the appropriateness of the question for the book you are evaluating.

Overall questions:

- Does the artwork extend or clarify the text?
- Does the artist make the viewer see something in a new way?
- Is the content of the illustrations appropriate for the book's purpose?
- Is the number of illustrations appropriate for the book's purpose?
- Are pictorial conventions from authentic cultural groups used to add realism to the content?

Color

- How is color used? Do the colors convey mood and emotions? Do the colors provide movement? Are they passively in the background?
- Are the colors appropriate for the text?
- What role does color play in the layout of the page?
- Are contrasting colors, tones, shades, and tints used to create variety, texture, and perspective?

Line

- Are lines used effectively?
- Are the lines strong and solid or diminutive and quick?
- Do they express movement?
- Does the width of the lines or crosshatching add perspective to the person or subject?

Shape

- Is shape handled effectively?
- Does shape help tell the story?
- How do shapes on the same page relate to each other?
- Is the page crowded and cluttered with shapes?

Composition

- Do the layout and size of the pictures carry the eye from page to page and create a rhythm in keeping with the meaning of the book?
- Is there a balance between the pictures and the text?
- Do the pictures and text create a pleasing effect?
- Is there variety and unity?
- Is there a focus to the illustration?

Design

- Is the choice of medium in keeping with the mood or the story or the concept being presented?
- Is the typeface appropriate to the book and the intended user?
- Is the paper in keeping with the original medium (acrylic on shiny paper, watercolor or pencil on a matte finish)?

EXAMINING WORDLESS BOOKS

In **wordless** books, the story line is told entirely with pictures or with a minimum of words. Wordless books vary in style and sophistication. Those for younger children have basic line drawings, crisp format, clear plots, and straightforward story lines. They require focus and unity, created through the illustrations and the format of the book. For older children, the artwork is more detailed and the themes are more highly developed and complex. For younger children telling the story in a wordless book can facilitate interactive experiences of several readers, two children or a child and adult. Such books provide basic cognitive exercises in sequencing and language development. Reading these books involves the literary elements of character, plot, setting, style, and theme. For older children wordless books can serve as a take-off point for creative writing.

Special Criteria

Questions to consider:

- Is action shown in each illustration?
- Does the story move from the familiar to the unfamiliar?
- Is the sequence of the action clear?
- Is the story line distinct?
- Is the information clearly developed?
- Do the illustrations clearly present the literary elements of character, plot, setting, style, and theme?

SUMMARY

Illustrations play a significant role in communicating the story or presenting information in picture books. Artists choose pictorial elements, decide on the composition of the illustrations, and select appropriate media to create unified works. Compatible book design can enhance the illustrations. In wordless books the illustrations must communicate both the visual and literary elements. Careful use of criteria can guide the evaluation of picture book illustrations.

TITLES MENTIONED IN THIS CHAPTER

The Alphabet Tale by Jan Garten, illustrated by Muriel Batherman. Greenwillow, 1994.

And Then What Happened, Paul Revere? by Jean Fritz, illustrated by Margot Tomes. Coward/McCann Putnam, 1973.

Animals of the Bible, text selected by Helen Dean Fish from the King James Bible, illustrated by Dorothy P. Lathrop. Lippincott, 1937.

Beware the Brindlebeast by Anita Riggio. Boyds Mills Press, 1994.

Big Fat Hen by Keith Baker. Harcourt, Brace, 1994.

Black and White by David Macaulay. Houghton Mifflin, 1990.

Color Zoo by Lois Ehlert. Lippincott, 1989.

Ginger Jumps by Lisa Campbell Ernst. Bradbury Press, 1990.

Good Night Gorilla by Peggy Rathmann. Putnam, 1994.

The Graphic Alphabet by David Pelletier. Orchard, 1996.

Have You Seen My Duckling? by Nancy Tafuri. Puffin, 1986, OP.

The Heart: Our Circulatory System by Seymour Simon. Morrow, 1996.

Hello! Goodbye! by Aliki. Greenwillow, 1996.

Letter Jesters by Carolyn Falwell. Ticknor & Fields, 1994.

Looking at Pictures: An Introduction to Art for Young People by Joy Richardson. Harry N. Abrams, 1997.

The Painter's Eye: Learning to Look at Contemporary American Art by Jan Greenberg and Sandra Jordan. Delacorte Press, 1994.

Pink and Say by Patricia Polacco. Philomel Books, 1994.

The Robber Baby: Stories from the Greek Myths by Anne Rockwell. Greenwillow, 1994.

Smoky Night by Eve Bunting, illustrated by David Diaz. Harcourt Brace, 1994.

Street Music by Arnold Adoff, illustrated by Karen Barbour. Harper/Collins, 1995.

Time Flies by Eric Rohmann. Crown, 1994.

A Tree is Nice by Janice May Udry, illustrated by Marc Simont (Paperback, Harper & Row, 1987) also available in Spanish, Un Arbol Es Hermoso (Harper Acro Iris, 1995).

The True Story of the Three Little Pigs by Jon Scieszka, illustrated by Lanc Smith. Viking 1992.

Tuesday by David Wiesner. Clarion, 1991.

REFERENCES

Anderson, Cheri. 1995. "The Role of Picturebook Illustration in Visual Literacy." *New Advocate* 8, no. 4 (Fall): 305–12.

Association for Library Service to Children. 1999. *The Newbery and Caldecott Awards: A Guide to the Medal and Honor Books* (Annual). Chicago: American Library Association.

Bader, Barbara. 1998. "American Picture Books from Max's Metaphorical Monsters to Lilly's Purple Plastic Purse." *Horn Book Magazine* 74, no. 2 (March/April): 141–156.

Cianciolo, Patricia J. 1990. *Picture Books for Children*. 3rd ed. Chicago: American Library Association.

———. 1997. *Picture Books for Children*. 4th ed. Chicago: American Library Association.

Cullinan, Bernice. 1994. "75 Authors & Illustrators Everyone Should Know." Children's Book Council. Brochure

Elleman, Barbara. 1995. "Illustration as Art: Character." *Book Links* 5, no. 1 (September): 34–37.

———. 1995. "Illustration as Art: Color." *Book Links* 4, no. 5 (May): 58–61.

———. 1995. "Illustration as Art: Line." *Book Links* 4, no. 3 (January): 54–57.

———. 1996. "Illustration as Art: Perspective." *Book Links* 5, no. 6 (July): 37–39.

———. 1996. "Illustration as Art: Shape." *Book Links* 5, no. 4 (March): 52–55.

———. 1994. "Illustration as Art: Techniques." *Book Links* 3, no. 5 (May): 28–31.

———. 1994. "Illustration as Art: Techniques, II." *Book Links* 4, no. 1 (September): 48–51.

———. 1994. "The Visual Connection." *Book Links* 3, no. 5 (May): 5.

Evans, Dilys. 1992. "Black-and-White Magic." *Book Links* 2, no. 1 (September): 49–53.

Harms, Jeanne McLain, and Lucille Lettow. 1996. "Book Design, Part I." *Book Links* 6, no. 2 (November): 52–54.

———. 1997. "Book Design, Part II." *Book Links* 6, no. 4 (March): 31–33.

Horn Book Magazine. 1988. "Picture Books: Special Issue." *Horn Book Magazine* 74, no. 2 (March/April).

Kiefer, Barbara. 1993. "Visual Criticism and Children's Literature." In *Evaluating Children's Books: A Critical Look, Aesthetic, Social, and Political Aspects of Analyzing and Using Children's Books*, edited by Betsy Hearne and Roger Sutton. Allerton Park Institute, no. 34. Urbana-Champaign, Ill.: Graduate School of Library and Information Science, University of Illinois.

Lucie-Smith, Edward. 1988. *The Thames and Hudson Dictionary of Art Terms*. New York: Thames and Hudson.

Milwaukee Public Library. Nd. "Let's Talk about Picture Books for Children." Milwaukee, Wisc.: Public Library.

Nodelman, Perry. 1988. *Words about Pictures: The Narrative Art of Children's Picture Books*. Athens, Ga.: University of Georgia Press.

Stewig, John Warren. 1995. *Look at Picture Books*. Fort Atkinson, Wisc.: Highsmith Press.

Williams, Barbara Osborne. 1994. "Every Picture Tells a Story: The Magic of Wordless Books." *School Library Journal* 40, no. 8 (August): 38–39.

Yenawine, Philip. 1995. *Key Art Terms for Beginners*. New York: Harry N. Abrams.

RECOMMENDED PROFESSIONAL RESOURCES

Carle, Eric. 1996. *The Art of Eric Carle.* New York: Philomel.
Includes autobiography, essays about his work, a step-by-step photo essay on his collage techniques; and samples of his illustrations.

Cummings, Pat, compiler and editor. 1992. *Talking with Artists.* New York: Bradbury, and 1995, *Talking with Artists, Volume Two.* New York: Simon & Schuster.
Succinct autobiographical sketches followed by questions and answers make this an informative and informal way to meet these illustrators. Includes photographs and reproductions of artwork.

Englebaugh, Debi. 1994. *Art through Children's Literature: Creative Art Lessons for Caldecott Books*. Englewood, Colo.: Teacher Ideas Press/Libraries Unlimited.
Suggests activities for teachers and librarians to help children understand the techniques used by the illustrators. Covers Award winners from 1938 to 1994.

Heller, Ruth. 1995. *Color*. New York: Putnam.
Explains colors and how they are created in the printing process.

Kehoe, Michael. 1993. *A Book Takes Root: The Making of a Picture Book*. Minneapolis: Lerner.

Also available in paperback. Straightforward text and informative photographs trace the process from the author's idea through the casing-in of the signatures to the covers. Terms are explained both in the text and in a glossary.

Kiefer, Barbara Z. 1995. *The Potential of Picture Books: From Visual Literacy to Aesthetic Understanding*. Englewood Cliffs, N.J.: Merrill.

Provides an informative discussion of how children look at picture books, how they respond to specific titles, and how to use picture books in the classroom. A glossary clarifies terminology for the nonartist.

Lacy, Lyn Ellen. 1986. *Art and Design in Children's Picture Books: An Analysis of Caldecott Award-Winning Illustrations*. Chicago: American Library Association.

Highly recommended for her sections on art appreciation for children using selected titles. Her comments vividly bring images from familiar titles to the reader and motivate one to reexamine them with new insight.

Marantz, Sylvia S. 1992. *Picture Books for Looking and Learning: Awakening Visual Perceptions through the Art of Children's Books*. Phoenix, Ariz: Oryx.

Offers guidelines and examples for introducing children to art through use of children's books.

Richardson, Joy. *Looking at Pictures: An Introduction to Art for Young People*. 1997. New York: Harry N. Abrams.

Takes the reader behind the scenes in the National Gallery in London. In the process shows various pictorial elements and techniques including color, use of light, and arrangement. The use of British spelling should not deter most readers.

Richey, Virginia H., and Puckett, Katharyn E. *Wordless Picture Books: A Guide*. 1992. Englewood, Colo.: Libraries Unlimited.

Includes explanation of terms for formats and different types of wordless books. Indexed by title, format, use of print, series, illustration, and subject. Arranged alphabetically by author. Entries provide author, reteller, translator, title, illustrator, publisher, date, International Standard Book Number (ISBN), Library of Congress Number (LCCN), series title, description of print use, format, and brief annotation covering plot or content and type of illustration used.

Shulevitz, Uri. 1985. *Writing with Pictures: How to Write and Illustrate Children's Books*. New York: Watson-Guptill.

Follows these steps: telling the story, developing a storyboard and book dummy, creating the pictures (covers, space and composition, techniques), and reproducing the art-work. His experience as a teacher of writing and illustration shows through.

Stewig, John Warren. 1995. *Look at Picture Books*. Fort Atkinson, Wisc.: Highsmith Press.

Discusses pictorial elements, composition, media, book design, and the influence of art movements on children's books.

Welton, Jude. 1994. *Drawing: A Young Artist's Guide*. New York: Dorling Kindersley.

Illustrates various pictorial elements and their effects. Offers suggestions for ways children can try the techniques.

Westray, Kathleen. 1993. *A Color Sampler*. New York: Ticknor & Fields. Using quilt patterns the author presents an introduction for pupils in grades two to five on how primary colors are mixed to make secondary and intermediate colors; how hues are created; and how pattern and juxtaposition create optical illustrations. Illustrates the effects of black, white, and gray on colors.

Yenawine, Philip. 1991. *Lines*. New York: Delacorte.

For grades two through five. Illustrates how artists use lines and the different effects they can create. Uses questions to involve the child in examining lines in the paintings. Other titles in this series using resources from the Museum of Modern Art, New York, include *Colors* (New York: Delacorte, 1991), *Shapes* (Delacorte, 1991), and *Stories* (Delacorte, 1991).

Yenawine, Philip. 1995. *Key Art Terms for Beginners*. New York: Harry N. Abrams.

Defines and provides illustrations for styles, media, and the processes of visual arts.

REPRESENTATIVE ILLUSTRATORS

Brett, Jan. Realistic illustrator of picture storybooks and folklore titles by others or herself. She is known for details in the central illustration as well as in the borders. Representative examples are *The Mitten* (Putnam, 1989) and *The Hat* (Putnam, 1997).

Brown, Marc. Author and illustrator of the believable character Arthur, an anteater. The series about Arthur, his friends, and his family provide easy-to-read text with colorful illustrations, humor, and on themes or situations familiar to a child. His other series include Rhymes and Dinosaurs. He works in several media, but prefers pencil with watercolor.

Browne, Anthony. English author and illustrator. He has been highly praised for his creativity and his concern for sensitive children. His *Tunnel* (Knopf, 1989) includes surrealist drawings. A current title is *Voices in the Park* (Dorling Kindersley, 1998).

Carle, Eric. Illustrator and author noted for his colorful tissue paper illustrations that are photographed after the layered papers are pasted to cardboard. His well-received and still beloved *The Very Hungry Caterpillar* (Philomel, 1981) exemplifies that style. In the biographical *Flora and Tiger: 19 Very Short Stories from My Life* (Philomel, 1997) he writes for older readers.

Cooney, Barbara. Illustrator and author whose pleasure in small living things is evident in her illustrations. Her trilogy (*Miss Rumphius* [Viking, 1982], *Island Boy* [Viking, 1988], and *Hattie and the Wild Waves* [Viking, 1990]) contains elements of her family history.

Crews, Donald. Author and illustrator of picture books. His earlier works include books with sparse text, bright colors, and a sense of motion, such as *Freight Train* (Greenwillow, 1978). Look for his self-portrait in *Night at the Fair* (Greenwillow, 1998). Here he uses watercolors, gouache paints, and darker colors.

Diaz, David. Illustrator who creates collage reflecting the setting of the story as in *Smoky Night* by Eve Bunting (Harcourt Brace, 1994). He frames each illustration. Look at his books to see how illustrators use line to express feelings and to focus the viewer's eye. Another book by this team is *Going Home* (HarperCollins, 1996).

Dillon, Leo and Diane. Illustrators who research the culture, settings, historical period, and artwork of an era to incorporate these aspects into their illustrations. Their work is diverse, reflecting use of a wide range of media and styles. For Katherine Paterson's *The Tale of the Mandarin Ducks* (Dutton, 1990) they studied *ukiyo—e* a type of Japanese art. In *To Every Thing There is a Season* (Blue Sky, 1999) they use a variety of styles.

Ehlert, Lois. Author and illustrator of picture books. Her background as a designer and graphic artist is evident in her books with their bright colors, interesting shapes, and varying layouts. Two examples are *A Pair of Socks* by Stuart J. Murphy (MathStart series, HarperCollins, 1996) and *Mole's Hill: A Woodland Tale* (Harcourt Brace, 1994).

Frampton, David. Known for his detailed woodcuts as seen in *My Son John* by Jim Aylesworth (Holt, 1994); *Whaling Days* by Carol Carrick (Clarion, 1993); and *Miro in the Kingdom of the Sun* by Jane Kurtz (Houghton Mifflin, 1996).

Goble, Paul. Author and illustrator who uses the beliefs of the Sioux, Cheyenne, and Blackfoot tribes for his stories. His bold watercolors sharpened by white space create striking compositions filled with motion. He provides references for his stories. For an example see *The Lost Children: The Boys Who Were Neglected* (Bradbury, 1993).

Hyman, Trina Schart. Illustrator known for her realistic and at the same time romantic, illustrations for fairy tales and other stories. Each page of text is enclosed by a border, such as flowers found in the setting of the story. A representative example is Howard Pyle's *King Stork* reissued with new illustrations by Morrow in 1998.

Lionni, Leo. Author and illustrator whose bold colors and textured illustrations deal with serious subjects such as individuality and honesty. For an example of his sophisticated collage and design see *An Extraordinary Egg* (Knopf, 1994).

Macaulay, David. Author and illustrator of picture storybooks and information books. His pen and ink, black and white *Cathedral* (Houghton Mifflin, 1973) demonstrates the integration of text and illustrations and goes beyond the structure to include the human community. In more recent works he uses watercolor in imaginary compositions as in *Shortcut* (Houghton, 1995). In all his works he encourages the reader/viewer to question why things look the way they do.

Pinkney, Brian. Illustrator who uses oil paints over scratchboard to create sweeping lines and repeated contours to express energy. Examples include *Dear Benjamin Banneker* by Andrea David Pinkney (Gulliver, 1994) and *The Dark-Thirty: Southern Tales of the Supernatural* by Patricia C. McKissack (Knopf, 1992).

Pinkney, Jerry. Illustrator whose works include African and African-American characters drawn from models. His care with facial expressions and body stances bring individuality to the characters. Examples include *Tanya's Reunion*, by Valerie Flourney (Dial, 1995) and *John Henry* by Julius Lester (Dial, 1994).

Say, Allen. Japanese-American illustrator and author who writes about the relationship between people from Asia and the United States. Examples of his work can be found in picture storybooks, folktales, and a biography *El Chino* (Houghton, 1990). His realistic watercolor paintings are framed to help the reader focus on the characters, such as in *Grandfather's Journey* (Houghton Mifflin, 1993).

Sendak, Maurice. Illustrator and author known for his classic *Where the Wild Things Are* (Harper, 1963), which revolutionized what is appropriate for children's books, and for his illustrations for Else Holmelund Minarick's "Little Bear" series. His *We Are All in the Dumps with Jack and Guy* (HarperCollins, 1993) combines two nursery rhymes to illustrate the problems of the homeless.

Sís, Peter. Illustrator and author whose works reflect the influence of his growing up in Prague, Czechoslovakia. Examples of his work include *Monday's Troll*, poems by Jack Prelutsky (Morrow 1996) and his *Starry Messenger* (Farrar Straus Giroux, 1996). In the latter he works Galileo's words and drawings onto each page.

Smith, Lane. Illustrator and author whose abstract-like oil paintings mixed with collage are seen in *Math Curse* by Jon Sciezka (Viking 1995). The team also did *The Stinky Cheese Man and Other Fairly Stupid Tales* (Viking, 1992) and created the Time Warp Trio chapter books.

Van Allsburg, Chris. Author and illustrator of the contemporary classic *The Polar Express* (Houghton, 1985), drawn using pastels. *The Polar Express* is an example of how his books involve a universal theme, in this case faith. Van Allsburg is known for his use of scale, perspective, and introduction of the unpredictable.

Wiesner, David. Picture storybook author and illustrator of the almost wordless *Tuesday* (Clarion, 1991). Known for his attention to detail, use of line, and proportions, which lead the viewer on an imaginative exploration of the subject. Another example is *June 29, 1999* (Clarion, 1992).

Wisniewski, David. Author and illustrator of *The Wave of the Sea-Wolf* (Clarion, 1994), which draws on the Tlingit (Indian nation of the Pacific Northwest) myth. He is known for his detailed three-dimensional cut paper illustrations. Other titles include *Golem* (Clarion, 1996), which includes a note about the history and social context of the story, and *Sundiata: Lion King of Mali* (Clarion, 1992).

Chapter 6

Selecting Fiction

But a good story is not meant to instruct us. Its purpose is to entertain us by its action and characters; at the same time, it gives us insight into people and how they think and feel, and enlarges our understanding.

—Rebecca J. Lukens,
Essentials of Children's Literature

EXAMINING NARRATIVE FICTION

A **fiction** book is a narrative product of the writer's imagination. Its purpose is to entertain and amuse. **Realistic fiction** refers to stories about people, animals, or objects set in current times (**contemporary realism**) or in the past (**historical fiction**). In both, believable characters exist in realistic settings facing problems appropriate for that time and setting. **Fantasy** refers to authors' imaginative stories about people, animals, and objects in settings outside of our daily lives.

As in adult fiction there are several subcategories of fiction for children: stories about adventure, animals, sports, mysteries, humor, school, and other common experiences. Since realistic fiction deals with everyday life the topics cover a wide range of life experiences. Topics that were once taboo in children's literature are treated openly, honestly, and with sensitivity by the more skillful authors. These topics include alcoholism, child abuse, divorce, death, drugs, cross-cultural changes, homelessness, single parent families, same sex parents, and interracial families.

The chief characteristics of fiction are

- discernible characters,
- developing characters,
- interrelationship of character and conflict,
- credible setting,
- realistic plot,
- particular point of view,
- unique style or tone in the telling of the story, and
- insight for the readers into personal problems and assistance in understanding their own feelings and those of other people.

Eliza T. Dresang and Kate McClelland predict that additional characteristics will mark fiction works in the future:

- Plots: multilayered, nonlinear, and nonsequential; various points of entry; ambiguous resolutions; provocation of further thought; and lacking traditional "happy ending."
- Characters: multiple or uncommon points of view; deeply personal expression; reflection of children's own voices; and focus on growth in inner resilience and on connections with adults or peers, usually nonparents.
- Settings: more likely to be specifically described, rather than generic; include heretofore uncommon or underrepresented places; and define home and family in a nontraditional way.
- Themes: universal ramifications, unlimited in their range of "acceptable" topics.
- Style/tone: innovative graphics will change interactive involvement of the reader. In some books, words and pictures may transform one another, become one another. (Dresang and McClelland, 1996: 44)

SPECIAL CRITERIA FOR COMPONENTS OF NARRATIVE FICTION

The interdependent elements of theme, plot, setting, characters, points of view, and style comprise a fiction work. The theme is the main idea or the central meaning of the story. The plot presents the action. The setting is where and when the action takes place. The characters are the people, animals, or inanimate objects that carry out the actions. The story is told from a point of view. Style is the manner in which the author says something.

Theme

Theme is the central idea of the story, what the story means. It reveals the significance of the action. Theme is a comment, observation, or insight about the subject of the story. In order to accept the theme, the reader must believe in the character and that the character could have the experience described in the story. Theme can be judged for its relevance, an external factor, and for its coherence, an internal factor ordering the parts of the book to form a sequential, cohesive whole. The theme may be remembered long after the details of the plot are forgotten

A theme may be explicit or implicit. An **explicit theme** may be stated by a character or flatly stated in the narrative. Such a flat statement may sound preachy. **Implied themes** are revealed through the characters' actions and reactions.

Books for younger children usually are limited to one primary theme. Older readers can handle the complexity of secondary themes that are usually linked to the primary theme.

Didacticism, or instruction, is not appropriate in fictional narratives written for children. These novels and short stories are designed to give pleasure and increase understanding rather than to instruct. The one area in which you may find didacticism in children's books is in science fiction titles in which the author is trying to explain new views and values.

Theme may be hard to identify in nonsense and fantasy stories with their treatment of illogical and inconsistent aspects of life. These books cause the reader to look at and begin to understand the order and disorder in life and how anomalies fit together.

CRITERIA

Questions to ask about theme:

- What is the theme?
- Does the story answer the question, "why"?
- How does the author present the theme?
- Is the theme relevant to the child's experiences and developmental stage?
- Is the theme universal, or has the author joined the bandwagon in responding to a current concern in society?
- Is the story coherent?
- Is the story internally consistent, creating a convincing and unified whole?
- Is it entertaining without being moralistic?
- Does the story provide a new perspective for the reader?
- Is the theme intrinsic to the story?
- Is the protagonist believable?
- Is that character's adventure one that leads the reader to accept the theme?

Plot

Plot involves the actions (what happens in the story), the story line (the sequence of events), and how the writer chooses these to present and resolve the conflict. Even in a time-sequence series of events, causality can turn a narrative into a plot. As characters act and react to conflicts, the plot grows. Plot answers the question "what if?" or "what will happen next?" For young readers, plot is the key literary element. Tensions move the story and hold children's interest.

The author can create several types of **conflict** and may use more than one in a story. The main character (**protagonist**) may face a conflict against

- self (internal conflict of feelings within the protagonist),
- nature (as seen in survival stories),
- a person (the antagonist), or
- society (the rules at one's school can represent society).

In some series the characters are minimally developed and the conflict carries the story. These books often have predictable plots, which appeal to the inexperienced reader. At the same time, this predictability can eventually become boring to more able readers. In more carefully crafted fiction the character is more fully developed, and the incidents occur because of the protagonist's personal traits.

The author may choose one of three basic **narrative structures**. One is dictated by a strictly **chronological** order, for example, time of day or days in the week, and for all characters. A second way is to arrange the events in one or more **progressive plots** in which the rendition of the event is dictated by dramatic structure: the conflict is introduced, a climax is reached, and the story ends with resolution of the conflict. This is the pattern of many folk tales. A third option is to use the **episodic structure** in which there is a conflict and resolution in each chapter linked to the other chapters by characters or theme.

The reader of **interactive fiction** books selects from several choices to determine the progress of the story. The reader makes the choice at the end of an episode.

To keep the story moving, the author may choose to use different action patterns: the cliffhanger, sensationalism, suspense, foreshadowing, and climax. **Suspense** raises anticipations and expectations about what will happen, when it will happen, why it happened, the solution of the problem, the outcome of events, and the well being of the character. Using suspense at the end of the chapter to set the stage for the next chapter is a device known as a **cliffhanger**. This is effective in stories for reading aloud to a group of children in several sittings. In **foreshadowing** the author provides clues to what will happen later on, providing a pattern of predictability. If the author does not relieve the suspense, the story becomes **sensational**. Adults might enjoy this in mystery stories and murder thrillers, but children may find it an uncomfortable form of tension.

The **climax** is the moment of high interest and may be the crisis or the turning point for the protagonist. Children may realize that this is the point where they knew how it was going to end. This resolution of the conflict is also called a **denouement**. When the twists and turns of the story have been unraveled and the reader finds a satisfactory ending, the plot has a **closed ending**. This type of conclusion is reassuring to young children. An **open ending** leaves the conclusion up to the reader.

CRITERIA

Questions one should consider about plot:

- How early in the story is the reader's interest captured?
- Docs the story have a beginning, a middle, and an ending?
- Does the beginning introduce the reader to the conflict?
- Does the author develop the story logically?
- Is the conflict developed in the middle of the story?
- Is the conflict resolved at the end of the story?
- Does the author use events to develop the action and unity of the story?
- Are the incidents determined by the local nature of events and consistent with the narrative?
- Do the incidents involve change and development with tensions and complications that are plausible but not predictable?
- Is the plot based on some element of novelty, surprise, or the unexpected?
- Is the movement of the story maintained?
- Will the pace of the story maintain the reader's interest?
- Is the plot structure appropriate for the intended audience?
- How does the author weave events, actions, conflicts, characters, and setting to develop the plot?
- Are the plot, setting, characters, and style consistently organized?
- Does the author catch the reader's interest in the beginning?

Setting

The term **setting** refers to when and where the story takes place and the descriptive details about the place of action. Setting can function to establish the mood of a story, to influence the lives of characters, or to provide local color. To test the importance of the setting to a specific story one can ask, "would this be the same story without this setting?"

There are two types of settings: backdrop and integral. The **backdrop setting** is like the scenery in a drama, it sets a place for the action but doesn't take a role in story. Different stories could be set against the same background. The

integral setting plays a more active role. Examples can be found in historical fiction, in which the setting clarifies a conflict, or in survival stories, in which the setting becomes the antagonist threatening the protagonist. The setting can also explain the character's beliefs and actions. If the author uses the setting as an integral part of the story, then the setting must be so clearly described that the reader is aware of the relationship. A one-dimensional setting, like a flat character, will not be as believable as a more fully developed setting in influencing the plot.

Functions of setting:

1. clarifies conflict
    a. in historical fiction gives reality to the story,
    b. in regional literature shows how time and place affect the story,
    c. in fantasy, author manipulates the description of the setting, to lengthening or shortening, simplifying or elaborating, as appropriate to the story
2. serves as antagonist in survival stories
3. illuminates character
4. acts as a symbol, such as good or evil found in folk tales

In picture storybooks the illustrations rather than the text may present the setting. Whether in text or illustrations, the setting must be consistent throughout the story.

CRITERIA

Questions to consider about setting:

*   Does the setting serve as a backdrop to the story, or does it play an integral role?
*   Does the setting contribute to the credibility of the action?
*   Is the setting one children will recognize or accept?
*   Does the description of the setting give a sense of the authenticity of the time period?
*   If the setting is an actual place is the description accurate?
*   Does the description of an imaginary place provide sufficient details to be a credible setting for that story?

Character

Character means a person, personified animal, or inanimate object whose actions and personal qualities are limited by that character's role in the story. The writer has the responsibility of making the main character believable. The character in the center of the conflict (the protagonist) will be developed more fully than one in the background.

Characterization refers to how the author reveals the characters. A **flat character** is not fully developed. In picture storybooks and in morals the character may have only one facet or personality trait. A **rounded character** is three-dimensional, with contradictions and realistic complexities. The character's traits are demonstrated in the action of the story. Character and action need to be unified; flat characters do not grow out of the action, rounded characters do. By the same token, action can stem from the rounded character but not from the flat one. Rounded characters are thus integrated with the action.

When a character has only a few traits and these are generally attributed to the social or racial group of which the character is a member, the character is called a **stereotype**. This type of stereotyping is misleading to the child reader, who may think this is a realistic description of the group portrayed. Another type of stereotype for a minor character is the **stock character**, who has a specific personality trait that is often used in other stories or has a specific role in society. Examples include a spoiled younger sister in a story or a trickster found in a folktale.

For young children, the protagonist might be a rounded character, with the secondary figures being flat characters. Books for older children include both major and minor characters with fuller development.

A story may have a **dynamic character** who changes as a result of the impact of the events. These changes can help the reader understand the action. A character who does not change is called a **static character**. Minor characters tend to be static. A minor character who is too fully developed can change the plot and cause the loss of unity that the author seeks between characters and plot.

Characterization is the method a writer uses to describe and reveal the characters. Authors use techniques such as action and dialogue to introduce characters. There are three common methods.

1. Directly describe the character,
2. Present the character in action, and
3. Reveal the character's thoughts and emotions.

The deft author is able to use action and speeches to reveal how the character and event result in changes. This creates a unity of character and action.

CRITERIA

Questions to consider about the characters in a story:

- Is the author's delineation of the character appropriate for the intended audience?
- Are the characters believable?

- Do the characters cause action?
- Do the characters grow and develop?
- Is at least one character fully developed?
- Is each character unique?
- Is the character's action appropriate for his or her personality?
- Do the characters represent universal qualities without becoming stereotyped?
- Can the reader identify with the actions, motives, and feelings of the protagonist?
- How does the author reveal the characters?
- Are the characters convincing in their actions?

Style

Style refers to how the book is written: how the author uses words to communicate ideas, establish moods, and anticipate understanding. As the illustrator uses pictorial elements, the writer uses literary devices. Styles vary from author to author and in the books of a particular author. Style can be simple or complex depending on the mood and setting of the story.

Styles can be examined in terms of

- arrangement of ideas
- choice of words
- use of figurative language
- structure and variety of sentences
- rhythm
- repetition of words and phases
- coherence of sentences, paragraphs, and chapters
- emphasis on words or passages
- unity of the parts: The source of unity may be plot, characterization, form, theme, mood, imagery, or symbolism.

The author chooses from the devices of style.

1. **Connotation**: the associations, images, or impressions that word brings to a reader; not the literal meaning of the word.
2. **Imagery**: an appeal to the senses (taste, smell, hearing, touch, sight) and to the reader's emotions
3. **Figurative Language**: use of figures of speech to create comparisons or associations, use of words in nonliteral sense
   a. **Personification**: attributing human traits to animals, plants, inanimate objects, natural forces, or abstract ideas
   b. **Simile**: use of *as*, *like*, or *as if* to directly compare two different objects, actions, or attributes that share some point of similarity

    c. **Metaphor**: implied comparison or identification of one thing with another without using the terms *as* or *like*

    d. **Hyperbole**: exaggeration or overstatement meant to create humor or emphasis, not to be taken literally

4. **Rhythm**: the patterned flow of sound. Writers use sound devices to contribute to the rhythm of the story, which is evident when the story is read aloud.

Diction, or word choice, is how the writer gives the flavor of the time, place, and events. This is found in history and regional works using language that appears to be of that period and locality. In high fantasy dignified language seems appropriate for the struggle between good and evil.

CRITERIA

Questions to consider about style:

- Does the author treat the young reader with respect?
- Does the author avoid using sentimental language, talking down to the reader, preaching, and oversimplifying?
- Is there a rhythm to the story?
- How does the author use words in relation to objects?
- What is the relationship among the words?
- Does the author use an objective or subjective style?
- What literary devices does the author use?
- Is the author's style accessible to children?
- Is the style appropriate for the subject?
- Is the dialogue natural?
- Is the use of language fresh and imaginative?
- Does the narrative flow easily?
- Is the style appropriate to the theme?
- Does the choice of words and syntax create a mood or help convey ideas?
- Does the author tell the story with sensitivity rather than in a sensational manner?

Point of View

Point of view refers to whoever is telling the story—the author or one of the characters. This perception of the action may be that of the first person (character as "I") or third person (he, she, they).

    Examples of point of view:

- First person: tells the story from inside the head of the character. This approach establishes credibility and brings a sense of intimacy between character and reader.

- First-person observer: a character not directly involved in the action tells what he or she observes using the first person "I."
- Author-observer: a third person tells about deeds, words, gestures in an objective manner without going into the minds of characters or offering the author's comments.
- Omniscient: the author, using the third person, relates every detail of action as well as the characters' conscious or unconscious thoughts and feelings. The omniscient narrator knows the present, past, and future, and sometimes comments on the actions of the characters.
- Combination: author may combine several of the above points of view through the use of dialogue, diary entries, and other techniques.

The author will vary the point of view depending upon subject matter, type of conflict, and maturity level of the intended readers. The third person form is the one most commonly used in children's literature.

CRITERIA

Questions to consider about point of view:

- Who is telling the story?
- Does the narrator have credibility in knowing that point of view?
- Is the point of view appropriate for the story?
- Is more than one point of view used and is there a reason for that change?
- Is the change in point of view one the reader can understand?
- If the author shifts the point of view between chapters what clues will help the reader to be aware of the change?
- Does the point of view give a perspective that is believable and that enriches the story?

Tone

Tone in literature tells us how the author feels about his or her subject, characters, and readers. Sentence structure, choice of words, word patterns or word usage, and arrangements all influence tone. Tone can be described as humorous, kindly, affectionate, pleasant, brusque, friendly, serious, lighthearted, mysterious, insinuating, and teasing. Different readers will respond to different tones in differing manners. The response will be based on their preferences and their experiences.

Certain tones used in adult literature are not as acceptable in children's literature. The ironic humor and wit in satire may be an intellectual exercise beyond children's experiences. They may lack the ability and maturity to see and interpret the irony, the understatements, the sarcasm, and the innuendoes.

When a writer creates a tearjerker situation that plays excessively upon the reader's sentiment, the results (**sentimentality**) evoke an exaggerated response. A writer who talks down to children with a condescending attitude is insulting and disrespectful of the child reader. Examples can be found in the retelling of folk literature and of the "classics." The overuse of sentiment is a form of condescension.

A **sensational** tone may occur in mysteries when a writer includes unnecessary and overly descriptive violence. Rebecca J. Lukens observes that "Like overused sentimentality, sensationalism may dull the reader's reaction to emotional pain or physical discomfort in real life" (Lukens, 1999: 236).

Another negative element is found in works where the author is deliberately preaching (**didacticism**). While this is not appropriate in works of fiction for children, clearly stated moral lessons are appropriate elements in fables.

EXAMINING CLASSICS

Another area of literature that raises questions is that of the classics. A **classic** is a book with permanence, one that remains a favorite for more than one generation of children. Children's classics are not adult classics, even watered-down versions. There are many children's books that are classics, and they are represented in all genres including historical fiction, high fantasy, and picture storybooks. Common characteristics are:

- strong, unique, credible characters
- engaging style
- appeal to children of more than one generation
- universal theme
- memorable story

In 1997 children in Seattle, Washington, were asked to write an essay about their favorite book. Some of the classics that appear on their lists are *Ramona the Pest* by Beverly Cleary, *The Hobbit* by J. R. R. Tolkien, *Charlotte's Web* by E. B. White, *The Lion, the Witch and the Wardrobe* by C. S. Lewis, and *Pippi Longstocking* by Astrid Lindgren. (De Leon, 1997: E 1–3)

EXAMINING SERIES BOOKS

There are two types of **series books** available in children's fiction: **formula series** and **literary series**. A common characteristic of both is one character who appears in several volumes. In the formula book, such as Nancy Drew, this character is flat and does not grow or develop. In the literary series, such as Beverly Cleary's Ramona books, the character is a rounded, three-dimensional person who grows and develops in the story. The formula books focus on a fast moving plot, while the literary series may have a thought-provoking theme. Some critics consider the formula books to be commercially driven, while the literary types reflect artistic vision. Both have appeal, provide quick reads, and have a minimum of description to slow them down.

One of the debates faced by people responsible for buying books for a school library media center collection is whether the monies should be spent on the formula series. The commercial nature of these works, where quantity is more important than quality, puts these titles in a different category from the literary series of "popular fiction" works. Familiar formula series include Nancy Drew, Hardy Boys, Babysitters Club, horror stories by R. L. Stine, and Animorphs. Although recognizing the limited literary merit of such works, some librarians argue that attracting developing readers is sufficient reason to have a limited number of these titles in the collection. Their predictability is satisfying for the inexperienced reader. One drawback is that many are available only in paperback editions that will not last for many circulations. However, these titles are popular with children, who recommend them to each other, so you can focus your book talks on leading children to the more literary titles.

Special Criteria for Series Books

Questions you should consider:

- Is the action fast paced?
- Is the plot logically developed?
- Does the book meet criteria for general fiction?
- Will this book fill a gap in the collection for developing readers?
- Will the book hold the reader's attention?
- Can this book be used as a stepping stone to books with more character development and more complex plots?
- Will the book physically withstand being read by a number of readers?

Additional criteria apply when one is evaluating the various subcategories of fiction. Discussion about picture storybooks, historical fiction, fantasy, animal stories, mysteries, and sports stories will be the subject of Chapter Seven.

SUMMARY

The purpose of fiction is primarily to entertain and amuse; to a lesser extent to instruct. Theme, plot, setting, and characters form interdependent elements. The author's style, point of view, and tone affect how the story is communicated.

Series books may be formula driven, or they can be more literary with characters who develop throughout the sequence of titles.

TITLES MENTIONED IN THIS CHAPTER

Charlotte's Web by E. B. White. HarperCollins, 1952.

The Hobbit; or, There and Back Again by J. R. R. Tolkien. Houghton Mifflin, nd.

The Lion, the Witch and the Wardrobe by C. S. Lewis. Macmillan, 1988.

Pippi Longstocking by Astrid Lindgren. Translated by Florence Lamborn. Viking, 1963.

Ramona the Pest by Beverly Cleary. Morrow, 1968.

REFERENCES

Bromley, Karen D'Angelo. 1996. *Webbing with Literature: Creating Story Maps with Children's Books* 2nd ed. Boston: Allyn and Bacon.

De Leon, Ferdinand M. 1997. "Winning Words." *The Seattle Times*, Section E (Monday, December 8): E 1–3.

Dresang, Eliza T., and Kate McClelland. 1996. "Radical Changes." *Book Links* 5, no. 6 (July): 40–46.

Elleman, Barbara. 1995. "Toward the 21st Century—Where are Children's Books Going?" *The New Advocate* 8, no. 3 (Summer):151–165.

Lukens, Rebecca J. 1999. *A Critical Handbook of Children's Literature*. 6th ed. New York: Longman.

Mackey, Margaret. 1990. "Filling the Gaps: *The Baby-Sitters Club*, The Series Book, and the Learning Reader." *Language Arts* 67 (September): 484–489.

Morner, Kathleen and Ralph Rausch. 1991. *NTC's Dictionary of Literary Terms*. Lincolnwood, Ill.: NTC Publishing.

Ross, Catherine Sheldrick. 1996. "Reading Series Books: What Readers Say." *School Library Media Quarterly* 24, no. 3 (Spring): 165–171.

RECOMMENDED PROFESSIONAL RESOURCES

Ansell, Janis and Pam Spencer. 1997. *What Do Children Read Next? A Reader's Guide to Fiction for Children*. Volume 2. Detroit: Gale Research.

This guide provides access to information about over 1,600 recent and classic juvenile titles for both avid and reluctant readers from grades one through eight. Entries provide bibliographic information, series name, age range, subjects (up to three themes or topics), major characters, when and where the story takes place, a brief plot summary, where it has been reviewed, other books by the author, and books on similar themes or in a similar style. Indexes are for awards, time period, geographic location, subject, character name, character description, age level, illustrator, author, and title.

Bauer, Marion Dane. 1992. *What's Your Story? A Young Person's Guide to Writing Fiction*. Boston: Houghton Mifflin.

Recommends young writers begin by writing a short story and offers practical advice for how to get started. Takes an honest approach to the realities of earning a living as a writer, but encourages writing for one's enjoyment.

Dresang, Eliza T. 1999. *Radical Change: Books for Youth in a Digital Age*. Bronx: H. W. Wilson.

Examines how literature is responding to the technological changes in society and how the technology is being used in that response.

Lukens, Rebecca J. 1999. *A Critical Handbook of Children's Literature*. 6th ed. New York: Longman.

Presents an in-depth discussion of literary elements in all genres of children's literature, including informational books. Lukens critically examines and evaluates a number of well-known titles.

REPRESENTATIVE AUTHORS

Blume, Judy. Author of the classic *Are You There, God? It's Me, Margaret* (Bradbury, 1970), which brought topics such as God and menstruation to children's books. Her first-person stories address contemporary personal concerns of her audience.

Cleary, Beverly. Author of contemporary fiction and known for her appealing characters, who face everyday situations with humor. Some of her characters (Henry, Ramona) have served as protagonists for their own series. Ramona, introduced in 1968, continues to appeal to young readers.

Conrad, Pam. Author of picture storybooks and fiction in which characters in historical or contemporary scenes cope with some kind of loss. Her suspenseful *Stonewords: A Ghost Story* was winner of the 1991 Edgar Allan Poe Award for Best Juvenile Mystery.

Danzinger, Paula. Author of the Amber Brown series (Putnam) and other chapter books. Writes funny stories about problems nine-year-olds face.

Fleischman, Paul. Author of picture storybooks, short stories, novels, and poetry. His characters face moral and psychological issues. His *Bull Run* (HarperCollins, 1993) is told through the voices of sixteen participants in the Battle of Bull Run. His *Joyful Noise* (HarperCollins, 1988), which is written to be read by two readers, is scientifically accurate.

Hamilton, Virginia. Writer of superb plots and vivid characters, whatever the genre. Her *M. C. Higgins, the Great* (Macmillan, 1974) is considered a classic by some writers. In *Her Stories: African American Folktales, Fairy Tales, and True Tales*, illustrated by Leo and Diane Dillon (Scholastic, 1995), she includes traditional folklore and "true tales". Her author's "Comment" about each story explains the sources or context of the story as well as terms or expressions used in the story.

Konigsburg, E. L. Author of novels, short stories, and picture storybooks. Her characters are strong and face inventive plots. She experiments with her writing style and point of view. *The View from Saturday* (Atheneum, 1996) is told from the point of view of each of four students telling their individual stories and their concerns about growing up.

Lowry, Lois. Author of the Anastasia series for young audiences and science fiction novels, such as *The Giver* (Houghton Mifflin, 1993), for older audiences. Her sense of humor and sensitivity to the human condition are ever present. Her characters develop as they face new and demanding situations. In *Number the Stars* (Houghton Mifflin, 1989), a story of the Danish Resistance told by a ten-year-old girl, she uses the last chapter as an "Aferword" to describe the fictional and factual details in the story. (As an aside, an excellent chapter to get children to think about the research that fiction writers do as they use their imagination to tell a story.)

MacLachlan, Patricia. Author of picture storybooks and fiction with a keen eye to familial relations whether in a contemporary or historical setting. Her *Sarah, Plain and Tall* (Harper, 1985) and its sequel *Skylark* (HarperCollins 1994) demonstrate how spare writing can have quality and be accessible to young readers of chapter books.

Naylor, Phyllis Reynolds. Author of fiction and nonfiction on a wide range of subjects. Her characters, whether mean or good, are vividly drawn. Her acute observation of human nature is evident in the trilogy of *Shiloh* (Macmillan, 1991), *Shiloh Season* (Atheneum, 1996), and *Saving Shiloh* (Atheneum, 1997).

Paterson, Katherine. Author whose realistic characters face difficult situations as they gain self-acceptance. This is evident in the 1978 Newbery Medal Award Winner *Bridge to Terabithia* (HarperCollins, 1977). In this contemporary realistic novel, Jess comes to terms with Leslie's accidental death. Other works by Paterson are historical in nature. For example, *Lyddie* (Dutton 1991) looks at the lives of the women who worked in the cloth factories of the 1840s.

Paulsen, Gary. Author of survival stories with narrow-escapes and near-death experiences as in his well-known *Hatchet* (Bradbury, 1987). His appreciation of the out-of-doors and of life as a farmer is found in *The Winter Room* (Orchard Books, 1989), in which he vividly describes the smells, sounds, and lights of farming days in the first half of the 20th century.

Rylant, Cynthia. Author of picture storybooks, poetry, novels, and the Henry and Mudge Ready-to-Read Series (Simon & Schuster). Her novels include fully developed characters exploring issues such as the necessity of grieving in *Missing May* (Orchard Books, 1992) or the reconciliation of one's religious beliefs with those of family and friends as in *A Fine White Dust* (Bradbury, 1986).

Simon, Seymour. Author of the "Einstein Anderson, The Science Detective" series (Morrow). These short stories use scientific facts for the solutions. Adam, called "Einstein," solves them with jokes and puns. See also information about Simon as a writer of science books.

Spinelli, Jerry. Author with a strong feel for language patterns, rhythms, and sounds. In his work for seven- to nine-year-old readers, the characters' conflicts are treated in a light hearted manner, see *Tooter Pepperday* (Random, 1995). In his works for older readers the conflict is more complex. In *Maniac*

Magee (Little, Brown, 1990) Jeffrey Lionel Magee (a half real, half legendary figure) faces racial tensions, death of a mentor, illiteracy, and family conflicts.

Voight, Cynthia. Author of realistic fiction, fantasy, and historical fiction with vivid descriptions of the setting and memorable characters. Readers were introduced to the Tillerman family in *Homecoming* (Atheneum, 1981), in which thirteen-year-old Dicey faced holding her three younger siblings together as a family after her mentally ill mother abandoned them.

Yep, Laurence. Author who draws on his Chinese and Chinese-American heritage in his historical works, such as *Dragon's Gate* (HarperCollins, 1993), an account of the roles of Chinese laborers in building the transcontinental railroad in the Sierra Mountains and in his realistic portrayal of cultural and generational conflicts in *Ribbons* (Putnam 1996).

Chapter 7

Selecting Genre Fiction

Novels can be viewed as cultural artifacts that simultaneously reflect and create society's values and concerns.

—Constance Burns,
"Middle-Grade Fiction."

EXAMINING GENRE FICTION

This chapter examines the characteristics and criteria for selecting narrative stories in the subcategories of picture storybooks, historical fiction, fantasy, mysteries, animal stories, and sports stories. These stories need to be evaluated both with general narrative criteria as well as with criteria specific to the genre. Representative authors are listed at the end of the chapter.

SPECIAL CRITERIA FOR GENRES

Picture Storybooks

In **picture storybooks** the pictorial and literary elements are of equal importance. The integration of illustrations and text creates a sense of unity. Barbara Bader describes their relationship.

> As an art form it [a picturebook] hinges on the interdependence of picture and words, on the simultaneous display of two face pages, and on the drama of the turning of the page. (Bader, 1976: [viii])

Strong illustrations may overpower a weak text; the reverse of these elements makes the opposite effect, i.e., a lack of complementing pictorial works weakens a strong text. Together the pictorial and literary elements should form an artistic unit unachievable separately.

The term **interactive book** pertains to titles often designed for children ages two to six. The child participates in the story in various ways. The text asks a question or suggests the child clap to the rhythm of the words, repeat a word or phrase, touch something, or look for specific objects. One example is *Have You Seen My Duckling?* by Nancy Tafuri, in which each double page spread provides an opportunity for the child to look for the missing duckling.

Picture storybooks often are housed in the "Easy" section of the library, which is misleading. The vocabulary may be at sixth- or seventh-grade reading level, while the interest level may be for anyone from very young children to adults. Picture storybooks are commonly 32 pages in length.

Characteristics of picture storybooks:

- Development of at least one round character
- Presence of action or tension
- Wide range of themes
- Settings integral with text and illustrations
- Told from a specific point of view
- Use of figurative language
- Range of tone

The protagonist is a rounded character who develops through interaction with the conflict. The character may be an anthropomorphic animal (an animal with human characteristics) that acts (perhaps also dresses) as a believable human being. Each character should have a relevant role to play in the story. Irrelevant characters can be confusing to young audiences.

As in stories for an older audience, one expects action or tension in picture storybooks. Mood pieces or character studies are less likely to hold the interest of young children than stories with an engaging plot.

There is a wide range of themes dealing with children's experiences. Certainly today's books reflect the diversity in our society. For example, newer definitions of the family exist; the typical family no longer is comprised of a mother, a father, two-and-a-half children, and their pets. Parenting today may be carried out by a grandmother, a single parent (male or female), a lesbian or gay couple, two sets of parents after a divorce and remarriage, a foster family, or with some other caregiver.

For humor to appeal to children, it should be broad and obvious. Adult-oriented humor should be avoided. However, it is also true that caregivers may be called on to read and reread the book, and they will need to be able to appreciate the humor as well.

In books dealing with intergenerational relations, look for books that challenge ageist stereotypes, books that explore the complexities of aging, and books dealing with death. Other common themes are a child's everyday experiences, growing up situations, attending school, and exploring nature.

Not all authors and illustrators use illustrations the same way. In some books text and illustrations are interwoven with the action, theme, and characters to create a setting. In other books, the illustrations handle all the descriptions of setting.

In writing the narrative, authors use the same range of options they do with other narratives. Examples can be found of the objective voice, the observer, the first person, and the omniscient point of view.

And, as with any other genre, styles vary. Authors may use figurative language to add imagery to the story. Some stories have a rhythmic quality that becomes most evident when the story is read aloud. Tone can range from thoughtful, serious, joyous, to humorous. The illustrations can enhance the tone.

CRITERIA

In evaluating picture storybooks one should apply the criteria used for literary merit (theme, plot, setting, characters, and style) plus those for pictures identified in Chapter 4.

Questions to consider about literary elements:

- Is the main character well rounded?
- Will the action maintain the young child's interest?
- Do the text and illustrations develop the theme?
- Do the text, the illustrations, or both describe the setting?
- Does the humor appeal to children?
- Does the author use clear, natural language?

Questions to consider about illustrations:

- Are the illustrations and text integrated rather than either one dominating the book?
- Are the details in the illustrations consistent with the text? Children will quickly spot differences.

Historical Fiction

Historical fiction is realistic fiction by a contemporary author about events set in an appropriate time period with characters true to that time. Imaginary characters and plot blend with the historical facts. Realistic language and appropriate dialogue are other important elements in historical fiction.

Characteristics of historical fiction:

- The setting represents a specific time period.
- The characters act and speak in a manner consistent with the time period, and they reflect the values of that period.
- Details about everyday life fit the time and place, if known.
- There is a credible problem, goal, or conflict.
- The plot or sequence of events are conceivable.
- The setting influences the plot.
- There is a universal theme or commonly shared truth.
- The story is told from an appropriate point of view or by a fitting narrator.
- The story is told with a unique style or tone.

It is particularly important that the actions of the characters reflect the standards and mores of the historical period. When actual historical figures appear in these novels, the author should include dialogue only when documentary evidence or other records can verify such activity. If a historical novel is narrated in the first person, the grammar, vocabulary, and sentence structure should authentically reflect the usage of the time period in which the book is set. Such language may be difficult for children to comprehend so, at times, the authors give the characters names of the period but use contemporary language.

The details of the setting should help the reader to visualize the time and place in which the events occur clearly. The setting should be authentic and accurately reflect historical and geographical data.

The concept of historical fiction can be confusing to a child. A book like Louisa May Alcott's *Little Women* was realistic fiction when it was written. However, for today's child it appears to be history. It is important to explain to today's reader that the author was not writing historical fiction; the values, opinions, and styles were real for the time in which the book was written because that was when the author lived. She was, in fact, writing about her own family.

CRITERIA

Questions to consider:

THEME

- Do the episodes in the story center on themes that adhere to facts?
- Does the author portray the "why" of the event?
- Do the issues of the past appear real to today's readers?
- Do the issues present an opportunity for explanations by parents, teachers, or school library media specialists?

PLOT

- Does the action reflect the pace of life in that historical period?
- Is the action and conflict resolution in keeping with the times in which the story is set?

SETTING

- Are time and place historically, geographically, and politically accurate?
- Is the setting authentic in terms of what we know about the history and geography at the time of the story?

CHARACTER

- Do the characters' characteristics, mannerisms, speech, dress, and attitudes reflect the historical period portrayed?
- Are the characters drawn convincingly as ordinary or extraordinary people who participated in these events?

STYLE

- Does the story convey a sense of life in that time period?
- Do the speech patterns sound right for the time period?

POINT OF VIEW

- Are fact and fiction blended in such a way that the background is subordinate to the story?
- Does the story reflect the values and spirit of the historical time?
- Does the author present the various points of view on issues of the times?
- Does the dialogue convey a feeling of the period without seeming artificial?

TONE

- Are notes, maps, time lines, bibliographies, and glossaries provided?
- Are the details of the time, place, and social order authentic?

Fantasy

Fantasy stories are realistic in most details, but they do require readers who are willing to suspend their disbelief about a character, theme, or setting. The characters may be personified animals or inanimate objects. In fantasy the key question of theme is frequently "What if?" This leads to "Then . . . ," that is, the consequences of the action. Finally, there is the answer to "So what?"—the meaning of the story.

Within fantasies by one author the reader will find the **cycle format**, in which one book is linked to another through characters, settings, or both. Some titles can be read independently of the others, but they make a fuller impact when the cycle is read in sequence. Cycle format readers enjoy knowing a specific character and following that character through other conflicts.

Science fiction is the subcategory of fantasy in which scientific laws and technological inventions play a key influence in the conflict and resolution. Science fiction often addresses the question "what if" by using scientific thought to explore the question or speculate about a world that could be.

In **high fantasy**, a subcategory of fantasy, the focus is on the conflict between good and evil. The reader judges the story in terms of its internal consistency within the imaginary world or by the protagonist's belief in his or her experience. Thus, point of view influences how the character is accepted. Settings may be the creation of the author, represent a more world-like location, or move back and forth between the two. The author may manipulate time, moving it back and forth. Themes often deal with universal questions about humanity. The tone is somber and in awe of the story. To be believable there must be a logic to the story, even if that logic is one perceived through a sense of humor rather than everyday rational behavior.

Characteristics of fantasy:

- Characters that include humanlike animals, stereotypes of good and evil, heroes and heroines with magical powers, or extraterrestrial beings
- A problem, goal, or conflict, sometimes between forces of good and evil
- A plot that may include adventures of the characters, or in science fiction, a heroic battle for the common good
- A climax, resolution of conflict, or accomplishment of the goal
- A theme or universal truth
- A clear point of view
- A tone or style that is special in some way

CRITERIA

Questions to consider about fantasies:

PLOT

- Does the story move from reality to the imaginative without breaking the credibility of the story?
- Are events interrelated?

THEME

- Does the story deal with a universal truth?
- Will the reader understand the symbolic significance of the theme?

SETTING

- Do the settings reflect originality on the part of the author?
- Is the setting appropriate for the story?

STYLE

- Does the author skillfully use words, phrases, symbols, and allegories to create images?
- Are the images credible?
- Do the supernatural aspects have credibility?
- Does the reader sense that the author has a creative imagination?
- For a science fiction story, is the story based on a scientific fact or hypothesis?
- Does a science fiction novel encourage consideration of the emotional, psychological, and mental effects of futuristic ideas, conflict, and change?
- Does the science fiction novel involve the reader in considering unlimited possibilities and in raising questions about other forms of life?

Mysteries

Mystery stories can be set in the present, the past, or the future. Suspense comes from unexplained events and actions, with an explanation or resolution by the end of the story. Plot is the key literary element in moving the story forward, and this high level of movement promotes fast reading. Characters may be flat, as in the formula series, or rounded and fully developed. The setting can be any locale. A popular feature for the regular mystery reader is the author's use of foreshadowing.

CRITERIA

Questions to consider:

- Is the tension created by unexplained events?
- Do the characters change because of the conflict?
- Does the action keep the plot moving?

Animal Stories

This subcategory includes stories in which animals behave like human beings, animals behave as animals but can talk, or animals behave as animals. Animals behaving as human beings are frequently found in picture storybooks for young children. In these cases the author uses **anthropomorphism** (assigns human behavior to the animal) so it becomes a believable character.

Authors can also present the animal behaving just like an animal. They show the reality of animal life by describing its natural habitat (weather conditions, geographical features); its life cycle; and the activities of its predators. Through these descriptions, the authors can explain the influence of these natural phenomena on the animal, and with these realistic elements they create tension in the story. It is with effective descriptions that authors can gain the reader's acceptance of the story.

In realistic fiction the author may choose to have the animal characters behave like animals. The author uses the observer point of view to create characters that seem real to the reader. For example, E. B. White in *Charlotte's Web* tells the story by having animals speak and think as humans but act like real animals.

CRITERIA

Questions to consider:

- Does the author use the observer point of view to create a realistic story?
- Does the author avoid being unrealistic and sentimental?
- Does the author's description of the setting add to the tension?
- Does the setting add credibility to the story?

Sports Stories

Well-developed characters and the author's style can add depth to a sports story. There are more books about team sports such as football, baseball, and basketball than about individual sports. While older sports stories focused on themes of team play and sportsmanship, more contemporary authors address themes dealing with racial harmony and gender-integrated sports.

CRITERIA

Questions to consider:

- Does the story have a theme beyond the winning of a game?
- Does the main character develop and grow because of events or conflicts in the story?

SUMMARY

Subcategories of fiction, including picture storybooks, historical fiction, fantasy, mysteries, animal stories, and sports stories, have unique characteristics. Books in these categories need to be evaluated using both the general criteria for all fiction works and the criteria unique to them.

TITLES MENTIONED IN THIS CHAPTER

Charlotte's Web by E. B. White. HarperCollins, 1952.
Have You Seen My Duckling? by Nancy Tafuri. Greenwillow 1984.
Little Women by Louisa May Alcott. Little, 1968.

REFERENCES

Bader, Barbara. 1976. *American Picturebooks: From Noah's Ark to the Beast Within*. New York: Macmillan.

Blos, Joan W. 1985. "The Overstuffed Sentence and Other Means for Assessing Historical Fiction for Children." *School Library Journal* 32, no. 3 (November): 38–39.

Burns, Constance. 1995. "Middle-Grade Fiction." In *Children's Books and Their Creators*, edited by Anita Silvey. Boston: Houghton Mifflin.

Cianciolo, Patricia J. 1997. *Picture Books for Children*. 4th ed. Chicago: American Library Association.

Elleman, Barbara. 1995. "Toward the 21st Century—Where Are Children's Books Going?" *The New Advocate* 8, no. 3 (Summer): 151–165.

RECOMMENDED PROFESSIONAL RESOURCES

Bader, Barbara. 1976. *American Picturebooks: From Noah's Ark to the Beast Within*. New York: Macmillan.
Comprehensive history of picture story books in the United States.

Holsinger, M. Paul. 1995. *The Ways of War: The Era of World War II in Children's and Young Adult Fiction*. Metuchen, N.J.: Scarecrow Press.
Annotated bibliography uses a rating system.

Lynn, Ruth Nadelman. 1995. *Fantasy Literature for Children and Young Adults: An Annotated Bibliography*. 4th ed. New Providence, N.J.: Bowker.
Annotated bibliography of novels and story collections for students in grades three to twelve. Also a guide to research articles, books, and dissertations. Excludes science fiction and horror literature.

REPRESENTATIVE AUTHORS

Berenstain, Stan and Jan. Authors and illustrators of the popular Bear family books and television programs. The family's activities are presented in a number of series aimed at different levels of reading, starting with "Bright and Early," and moving through "Berenstains' Beginner Books," "First Time Books," and "Big Chapter Books."

Bunting, Eve. Prolific writer of picture storybooks and novels that deal with a wide range of topics including social issues and classroom situations. Her *Coffin on a Case* (HarperCollins, 1992) won the best Juvenile Mystery Edgar Award in 1993. Her *Smoky Night* (illustrated by David Diaz, Harcourt Brace, 1994) is about the Watts riot. In *Train to Somewhere* (illustrated by Ronald Himler, Clarion, 1996) she writes about the orphan trains that took 100,000 homeless New York City orphans to the Midwest for possible adoption. In *Going Home* (illustrated by David Diaz, HarperCollins, 1996) the story deals with a Mexican family of farm laborers who return to Mexico, which the parents consider home.

Cooper, Susan. Author of fantasy, who in her writing for children is known for the fantasy sequence *The Dark Is Rising* (Atheneum, 1973), which deals with the eternal struggle between good and evil. Her *Boggart* (Macmillan, 1993) merges the world of supernatural with that of computer buffs.

Fleischman, Sid. Author and humorist of American tall tales and historical novels. The *"McBroom"* series represents his humorous writing for third through sixth grades. *The Whipping Boy* (illustrated by Peter Sís, Greenwillow, 1986) demonstrates his handling of themes like friendship, courage, and humor in a historical setting.

George, Jean Craighead. Author whose fiction and information books focus on human interaction with animals and natural environments. Her works include *Julie of the Wolves* (HarperCollins, 1973) and its sequels, ecological mysteries, and the One Day in . . . series of information books about environments.

Henkes, Kevin, author and illustrator known for his picture storybooks of mice characters (Lilly, Owen, Wendell, Sophie) with their human feelings and relationships. His ability to capture feelings is also evident in his fiction works such as *Sun and Spoon* (Greenwillow, 1997).

Hurwitz, Johanna. Author of humorous books about everyday life for readers in second though fifth grade. Familiar characters like Nora appear in more than one story. The setting is usually an urban apartment or a school.

Jacques, Brian. British author of the multivolume fantasy cycle set around Redwall Abbey. Fans of this community of animals and their many adventures are not deterred by the detailed descriptions or by the length (350 pages) of the novels.

Joyce, William. Author and illustrator whose works reflect his being a fan of movies, cartoons, and comics. His *Santa Calls* (HarperCollins, 1993) includes battles with the Dark Queen and her Dark Elves. *Bentley and Egg* (HarperCollins, 1992) is an adventure told from the perspective of a frog.

Keller, Holly. Author and illustrator whose picture storybooks have humor and memorable characters facing typical childhood situations. Representative titles are *Brave Horace* (Greenwillow, 1998) and *Geraldine First* (Greenwillow, 1996).

McCully, Emily Arnold. Illustrator and author of picture storybooks, such as *Mirette on the High Wire* (Putnam 1992), *Starring Mirette & Bellini* (Putnam, 1997) and a series about the theatrical Bear Family (HarperCollins). *The Pirate Queen* (Putnam, 1995) is based on facts and Irish legends.

McKissack, Patricia. African-American teller of folklore, stories, biographies, and information books who sometimes coauthors information books with her husband, Frederick McKissack. An example of their joint efforts is *Christmas in the Big House, Christmas in the Quarters* (Scholastic, 1994). In *The Dark-Thirty: Southern Tales of the Supernatural* (Knopf, 1992) she opens each story with a note about the story's background, setting, or the events of the period.

Polacco, Patricia. Author and illustrator of crosscultural friendships as in *Pink and Say* (Philomel, 1994), which is based on the friendship of a young black soldier with Polacco's great-great-grandfather in a Civil War battle. Other stories and illustrations reflect her Russian heritage and Ph.D. in art history, for example *Babushka Baba Yaga* (Philomel, 1993).

Soto, Gary. Author who draws on his Mexican American background for his children's books. His *Chato's Kitchen* (illustrated by Susan Gucvara, Putnam, 1995) is typical of his works in that it includes a glossary of Spanish words and phrases. His characters represent middle class and the economically disadvantaged, but their experiences are universal.

Steig, William. Author and illustrator who has received recognition for both his text and his illustrations. His consistent style of thick sketchy black lines with added watercolor are found in *Zeke Pippin* (HarperCollins, 1994) and *The Toy Brother* (HarperCollins, 1996)

Viorst, Judith. Author and poet with a sense of humor as seen in her book titles and stories. Examples include *Alexander, Who's Not (Do You Hear Me? I Mean It!) Going to Move* (Atheneum, 1995) and *Sad Underwear and Other Complications: More Poems for Children and Their Parents* (Atheneum, 1995).

Yolen, Jane. Author of fantasy, fiction, literary fairy tales, poetry, and picture storybooks, whose audiences range from very young children to young adults. Her works are imaginative and poetic. Representative titles are *Owl Moon* (illustrated by John Schoenherr, Philomel, 1987) and *Camelot: A Collection of Original Arthurian Stories* (Philomel, 1995).

Chapter 8

Selecting Folk Literature

Folklore . . . reflects a people's concept of themselves—their beliefs, hopes and fears, courage and humor, sense of delight in the odd, fascination with the supernatural. By its nature, folklore incorporates the traditional with a society's changing view of itself.
—Sara Miller, "American Folklore."

EXAMINING FOLK LITERATURE

The term **folklore** refers to the beliefs, manners, customs, observations, superstitions, tales, ballads, proverbs, music, and art of an earlier time. **Folk literature** refers to stories with uncertain origins that were handed down orally from one storyteller to another. This body of traditional narratives includes animal tales (*pourquoi* or "why" stories, trickster tales), fables, folktales, humorous tales (drolls, noodleheads, sillies, and numbskull tales), legends, myths, parables, tall tales, and traditional fairy tales. As M. Gail Hickey observes it is

> Through the tales, [that] we learn about a people's history, geography, sociology, language, music, literature, values, cultural mores and ethnic heritage. (Hickey, 1995: 13)

And

The interdisciplinary nature of folktales also makes them especially well-suited for thematic units centered around key social studies concepts. (Hickey, 1995: 13)

Folktales can also present another aspect of a culture: its printed language. For example, *The Rabbit's Judgment* by Suzanne Crowder Han has a bilingual text: English and Korean.

In the United States we find many of our tales are translated from another language. Bette Bosma points out that:

> In fact, the only tales that originated in English are the American regional and tall tales. American Indian myths and legends were first told or written down in tribal language. (Bosma, 1987: 7)

We need to make children aware of this interesting situation.

These traditional tales are different from those found in the fiction section of libraries. These are **literary fairy tales** written by known authors. Many of Hans Christian Andersen's tales fall in this category. Such writers create a story following the forms and elements of the traditional literature.

The writers of the folk literature (traditional stories) are known as **adapters** or **retellers**. They did not create the story; they made an old story available to us through their adaptation or retelling.

A careful writer provides **source notes** to describe the origin of the story and the changes made. Common changes include altering the motif or mood of the story and simplifying or elaborating the original version. Compilers who gather stories together also provide source notes about the background of the stories. Often information about the origin of the story may also be found on the inside flap of the book jacket and on the copyright page.

A collection of folklore may include **variants** of the same story. In this case, each of the stories shares common elements, such as the plot or character, but may have different settings or motifs. For example, there are many variants of the Cinderella story from around the world. Cinderella may have a different name in the stories, but the plot or a variation on it is the same.

Folktales

Folktales have common tripartite structure: construction (introduction), struggle (development of the story), and major climax (the conclusion).

1. Construction
   A few sentences introduce the main characters, the setting of the story, and the conflict to be solved. Conventional openings include "once upon a time," "long ago and far away," "in olden times when wishing still helped

one," "a thousand years ago tomorrow," and "once in a time, and a very good time too." A brief sketch of the scene lets the reader know where the action will take place. The objectively stated conflict alerts the reader to the magnitude and intensity of the challenge.

2. Struggle

In the middle section the quest begins, tasks are initiated and performed, and obstacles appear. The action mounts steadily until it reaches a climax. The plot is full of suspense and action. Fast action is a major characteristic of a folktale. The use of motifs can add to the suspense, as the reader or listener looks for the familiar pattern.

3. Major Climax

The last part is as brief as the introduction and completes all that was stated in the introduction. Conventional endings include "and they lived happily ever after"; "if they haven't left off their merry-making yet, why, they're still at it"; "a mouse did run, the story's done"; and "no one need ask if they were happy."

CHARACTERISTICS

Motif, the smallest part of a tale that exists independently, often reoccurs three or seven times in a story, although four times is characteristic of Native American tales. Common motifs are magical powers, transformations, magic objects, wishes, and trickery. The reteller creates repetitive story patterns by repeating a refrain or episode. As the reteller embellishes with new ideas or episodes and repeats what has gone before, the story becomes cumulative. These characteristics help children learn to anticipate what might happen. The comparison of motifs in folk literature is one method of introducing children to cross-cultural studies.

Many folktales have themes. The same theme can be found in the literature of more than one culture, as themes tend to state a universal truth. The reader readily sees the implicit theme through the characters and the conflict.

Characters in folktales are not developed individuals. Flat characters representing good and evil ones are easily recognized, and stock characters, like a trickster or a wicked stepmother, are frequently used. The teller may use a brief phrase to describe the character and repeat it frequently. These character descriptions cannot be long because the action in a folktale moves so quickly. Folktales are normally told in the third person. The tone of these stories may vary from humorous to sentimental, or they may be matter-of-fact.

Characteristics of folktales:

- Words capture sound and rhythm of oral language.
- Characters are easily recognized as good or bad.
- Brief phrases describe character.

- Stock characters appear frequently.
- Series of episodes maintain a quick flow of action.
- Narrator uses dialogue.
- Figurative language of metaphors and similes creates vivid images.
- Narrative patterns are predictable.
- Language is simple but full of rhythm and melody.
- Conflict is often between personified animals as well as people in "person-to-person" conflicts.
- Action has the inevitable conflict and resolution.
- Story ends briefly.
- Story has universal appeal and deals with common needs of people regardless of culture.
- Language uses idioms that reflect dialect or speech patterns of a particular region or people. (Children may need help in understanding idioms and learning not to read them literally.)

Animal tales consist of animals that act and talk like human beings with exaggerated human characterization. While the tales teach a lesson, they are not as didactic as fables.

The **humorous tales** (drolls, noodleheads, sillies, and numbskulls tales) revolve around a character who makes funny mistakes.

Pourquoi or **etiological** animal tales explain the "why" of natural phenomena, basing the explanation on animal traits or characteristics and customs of people. Unlike legends, these tales were meant to entertain, not to instruct their listeners.

Beast tales or **trickster stories** feature one character that is a trickster in animal shape. The coyote, the raven, Anansi the spider, and Reynard the fox often play this role.

Fables

A **fable** is a brief, didactic tale in which an animal or inanimate object speaks in human language and represents different aspects of human nature. A significant act is used to teach a moral or lesson. The setting is the backdrop for the stated moral.

Western culture has Aesop's fables, which were reportedly told by the Greek slave about 600 B.C. Familiar proverbial phrases, such as "sour grapes", or "a wolf in sheep's clothing" summarize the moral of well-known fables. From Eastern culture come the Jataka tales, or moralistic lessons involving the reincarnation of Buddha as an animal or bird, which have been recorded since 500 B.C. English versions often do not include the moral or teaching verses.

Other characteristics of fables:

- three or fewer characters
- single-trait characters

- single-incident plot
- no interpretation of action by narrator
- didactic purpose
- crisp, straightforward style
- abstract idea expressed in relatively few words
- implicit or explicit moral
- moral statement at end of story
- backdrop setting for the action

A **parable** has similar characteristics, but the main character is a human being. These brief stories deal with a moral or spiritual truth.

Myths

Myths, like legends, are stories told as if they were facts. They represent beliefs about supernatural forces and are told with dignity and simplicity. Myths

- explain the origin of man and of the world.
- interpret natural phenomena.
- explain religion.
- explore the meaning of life and death.

The characters in myths are gods, goddesses, and supernatural powers. The plots usually involve a single incident or a few incidents that are linked by the characters. They deal with issues of ethics and are full of strong emotions.

For Norse myths, Alexandra N. Leach comments that "One of the finest works is . . . Padraic Colum's *The Children of Odin: the Book of Northern Myths,*" published in 1920 by Macmillan, which at the time of this writing is out-of-print. However, this serves as a reminder that some old titles in a collection are still useful.

Common types of myths:

- **Creation myths**, or the various ways in which people explained creation
- **Nature myths**, explaining natural phenomena such as changes in seasons, characteristics of animals, earth formations, astronomy.
- **Hero myths**, in which the hero who accepts a dangerous assignment may be assisted or hindered by the gods, but the person remains the focus of the story.

Legends

Legends are tales about a specific historical event, person, or place presented as fact. The characters can be humans, animals as humans, and supernatural creatures. Some characters, such as Johnny Appleseed, are based on real people. Others, like Paul Bunyan, were invented. The setting is in a historic time and the place is a recognizable world. These stories involve change in creation and heroic deeds.

Tall Tales

Tall tales are highly exaggerated accounts of exploits. These hilarious tales involve careful detail and are based on reasonable activities. The language uses vivid vernacular idioms, dialect, and fanciful metaphors.

Common characteristics of tall tales:

- people (real or imagined)
- events (real or imagined)
- subjects that include hunting, agriculture, marvelous feats of strength or speed, or virtues of a place

Fairy Tales

Fairy tales are imaginary tales that involve enchantment, supernatural elements, or magical powers. The term fairy is misleading because there are not necessarily any fairies mentioned in the story. Common characteristics of fairy tales:

- elements of magic or enchantment in characters, plots, or settings
- use of magic objects or words to weave their enchantments
- opening and closing conventions such as "Once upon a time" and "they lived happily ever after"
- predictable patterns in which love, kindness, and truth prevail, and hate, wickedness, and evil are punished
- characters like fairies, elves, pixies, brownies, witches, magicians, genies, and fairy godparents
- characters that are all good or all bad
- quickly delineated flat characters
- vague settings

Modern humorous tales include **fractured fairy tales**, a genre that Julie Cummins describes as classic folk or fairy tales rewritten with tongue-in-cheek or as a spoof, using twists and spins on the original story's features. The text and visual references poke fun at the original, resulting in a witty, clever, and entertaining tale. (Cummins, 1997: 51) She cites *The True Story of the Three Pigs* (Viking 1989) by Jon Scieszka, illustrated by Lane Smith, as a classic in this genre. In this version, the wolf tells his view of the events.

Selection criteria for fractured fairy tales:

- Is it written for children?
- Does it use homor that children enjoy?

- Does it follow criteria for other good writing?
- Can one say that it "doesn't belittle the original source in its approach" (Cummins, 1997: 51)?

SPECIAL CRITERIA FOR ANTHOLOGIES

To select collections of folk literature, consider the following questions:

Purpose

- What is the purpose of the collection?
- Is the purpose stated in the introduction or in an opening section of the book?
- Does the purpose fill a need in the school library media center's collection?
- Is there a description of how and why the tales were selected?
- Do the tales meet the purpose of the anthology?
- Is there a theme or setting that is common to all the tales?
- How does the compiler or reteller relate the stories to each other?

Authority

- Is there evidence of the reteller and the illustrator's scholarship and attention to authenticity?
- Do source notes provide background information about the original versions of the stories?
- Is there an explanation of what changes were made and why?
- Is there information about variants of the tales?
- Do background notes describe the cultural context of the tales?

Style

- Is the narrative style preserved?
- Do the tales sound as if they were being told?

Audience

- Were the stories selected for the child reader or the adult storyteller?
- Are the selections appropriate for the intended user?
- Will the size of the book and the illustrations make this a useful book for reading aloud with a group?

Scope

- How many tales are included?
- What types of folktales are included?
- Is the collection limited to folk literature from one nation or ethnic group or representative of many sources?

Organization

- How are the stories arranged and organized?
- Does the organization help relate one story to another?
- Can the stories be read either independently or continuously?

Illustrations

- Do the illustrations enhance the tales?
- Does the artwork represent the country or culture of the tale's origin?
- Are the illustrations integral to the story or are they merely decorative?
- Are the illustrations placed appropriately?

Special Features

- Does the introduction provide guidance for using the anthology?
- Can a reader locate tales by title, source, motif, subject, or country of origin?
- Is there a table of contents?
- Are there one or more indexes?
- Does the book contain additional information that will be of use in the curriculum such as the genealogy of the gods or a glossary of names?
- Are there commentaries about the tales?
- Is the source of each tale identified?
- Do the acknowledgments and copyright information sections provide more information about the tales?
- Does the subtitle or author's note identify the particular type of story, such as myth, legend, or fable?

SPECIAL CRITERIA FOR A SINGLE STORY

General criteria apply to any type of folk literature. For tales published in a single story format, the following questions can be used.

- Is the story unique?
- Is the story for the child reader or the adult storyteller?
- Do the characters use figurative language and imagery? If dialect is used, is it accessible to children?
- Does the dialogue use everyday language?
- Does it sound as though a storyteller told it?
- Does the reteller give the origin of the story?
- Does the reteller explain how this version is a variant of others?
- Does the story remain true to the values, life-styles, and beliefs of the original culture?
- Does the language maintain the flavor of the country where the tale originated?
- Are the illustrations culturally accurate?
- Is the book a showcase of an artist's work or a new interpretation of the story?
- How does this version compare with others?

A representative list of tales published individually is provided at the end of this chapter.

SUMMARY

Traditional folk narratives, including folktales, fables, myths, legends, tall tales, and fairy tales, have unique characteristics. When selecting these stories one should consider the criteria for the book with a single story, for anthologies, or for collections of several stories.

TITLES MENTIONED IN THIS CHAPTER

The Children of Odin: The Book of Northern Myths by Padraic Colum. Macmillan, 1920.

The Rabbit's Judgment by Suzanne Crowder Han, illustrated by Yumi Heo. Holt, 1994.

The True Story of the Three Pigs by Jon Scieszka, illustrated by Lane Smith. Viking, 1989.

REFERENCES

Bosma, Bette. 1987. *Fairy Tales, Fables, Legends, and Myths: Using Folk Literature in Your Classroom*. New York: Teachers College, Columbia University.

Cummins, Julie. 1997. "Fractured Fairy Tales: Spin-Offs, Spoofs, and Satires." *School Library Journal* 43, no. 10 (October): 50—51.

Dooley, Patricia. 1994. "Beyond Cultural Literacy: The Enduring Power of Myths." *School Library Journal* 40, no. 6 (June): 52–53.

Green, Thomas A., ed. 1997. *Folklore: An Encyclopedia of Beliefs, Customs, Tales, Music, and Art*. Santa Barbara, Calif.: ABC-Clio.

Hearne, Betsy. 1993. "Cite the Source: Reducing Cultural Chaos in Picture Books, Part One." *School Library Journal* 39, no. 7 (July): 22–27.

———. 1993. "Respect the Source: Reducing Cultural Chaos in Picture Books, Part Two." *School Library Journal* 39, no. 8 (August): 33–37.

Hickey, M. Gail. 1995. "Focus on Folk Tales." *Social Studies and the Young Learner* 8, no. 2 (November/December): 13–14.

Jones, Alison. 1995. *Larousse Dictionary of World Folklore*. Edinburgh: Larousse.

Leach, Alexandra N. 1996. "Norse Mythology." *Book Links* 6, no. 2 (November): 9–14.

Miller, Sara. 1995. "American Folklore." In *Children's Books and Their Creators*, edited by Anita Silvey. Boston: Houghton Mifflin, 22–24.

Sachs, David. 1996. "Breathing New Life into Ancient Greece and Rome." *School Library Journal* 42, no. 11 (November): 38–39.

RECOMMENDED PROFESSIONAL RESOURCES

Blatt, Gloria T. 1993. *Once Upon a Folktale: Capturing the Folklore Process with Children*. New York: Teachers College, Columbia University.
Includes essays and activity suggestions about finding and using folklore with children.

Bosma, Bette. 1987. *Fairy Tales, Fables, Legends, and Myths: Using Folk Literature in Your Classroom*. New York: Teachers College, Columbia University.
Includes lesson plans designed to help children develop reading skills, analyze types of folktales, and engage in creative activities. Includes annotated listing of 142 folktales with descriptions of the story and suggested activities.

Helbig, Alethea K. and Agnes Regan Perkins. 1997. *Myths and Hero Tales: A Cross-Cultural Guide to Literature for Children and Young Adults*. Westport, Conn.: Greenwood Press. Indexes 1,455 stories for elementary through high school students by writer and book title. Identifies the general cultural area of the story (Native American rather than individual tribe unless so indicated in the book indexed); type of book (anthology, collection, single story); and whether a myth and hero story. Indexes types of stories by subject matter and format. Provides brief critical annotations of the books.

Sprug, Joseph W., compiler. 1994. *Index to Fairy Tales, 1987–1992: Including 310 Collections of Fairy Tales, Folktales, Myths, and Legends: With Significant pre-1987 Titles Not Previously Indexed.* Metuchen, N.J.: Scarecrow.
Continues *Index to Fairy Tales, 1978–1986* compiled by Norma Olin Ireland and Joseph W. Sprug. Provides access to stories by title, subject, author and, for a majority of the titles, themes as identified using the Thompson *Motif Index* number.

REPRESENTATIVE SINGLE TALE BOOKS

Barnes-Murphy, Frances, reteller. 1994. *The Fables of Aesop,* collected and illustrated by Rowan Barnes-Murphy. Lothrop, Lee & Shepard. 1994.
Includes table of contents, collector's note, information about Aesop, and title index.

Hurwitz, Johanna, selector. 1994. *A Word to the Wise and Other Proverbs*, illustrated by Robert Rayevsky (Morrow, 1994).
Juxtaposes proverbs so their meanings cancel each other out.

Kerven, Rosalind, reteller. 1998. *King Arthur* (Eyewitness Classics) illustrated by Tudor Humpries. Dorling Kindersley and *Aladdin* (Eyewitness Classics) illustrated by Nilesh Mistry. Dorling Kindersley.

Sutcliff, Rosemary. 1993. *Black Ships before Troy: The Story of the Iliad*, illustrated by Alan Lee (Delacorte, 1993)
Uses straightforward telling with realistic watercolors.

Talbot, Hudson. First in series: 1991. *King Arthur: Sword in the Stone.* Second in series: 1995. *King Arthur and the Round Table.* Third in series: 1996. *Excalibur.* Morrow.

REPRESENTATIVE AUTHORS, RETELLERS, AND ILLUSTRATORS

Aliki. (Brandenberg, Aliki.) Aliki's Greek heritage is evident in this book. *The Gods & Goddesses of Olympus* (HarperCollins, 1994). In her nonfiction works, she uses comic-strip style illustrations to help with explanations such as *My Visit to the Zoo* (HarperCollins, 1997). The people in her books represent the diversity in our country including those with physical limitations. She also writes and illustrates works of fiction and books explaining concepts, for example, *Hello! Good-Bye!* (Greenwillow, 1996). Some of her books are in the "Let's-Read-and-Find-Out" series (HarperCollins).

Barnes-Murphy, Frances, reteller. 1994. *The Fables of Aesop,* collected and illustrated by Rowan Barnes-Murphy. Lothrop, Lee & Shepard, 1994.

Bruchac, Joseph III. Native American author who draws on his heritage as he uses the direct language of a storyteller and provides background information about the stories. Representative titles include *The Boy Who Lived with the Bears* illustrated by Murv Jacob (HarperCollins, 1995) and *Flying with the Eagle, Racing the Great Bear: Stories from Native North America* (Bridgewater, 1993). His biography of Sitting Bull is titled *A Boy Called Slow*, illustrated by Rocco Baviera (Philomel Books, 1994).

Colum, Padraic. Irish author and adapter of folktales and legends. His book *The Trojan War and the Adventures of Odysseus* was reprinted in 1997 (Books of Wonder, Morrow) with illustrations by Barry Moser.

dePaola, Tomie. Illustrator and author of folklore, religious books, and picture storybooks. De Paola has recognizable characters and uses the folk style for his art work. Sample titles include *Days of the Blackbird: A Tale of Northern Italy* (Putnam, 1997); *Christopher: The Holy Giant* (Holiday House, 1994); and *Strega Nona: Her Story as Told to Tomie dePaola.* (Putnam, 1996).

Goble, Paul. Author, illustrator, and reteller of Plains Indian tales, including several tales about the spider trickster Iktomi (*Iktomi and the Buzzard* [Orchard Books, 1994]). He uses bold colors and lots of white space. Goble writes about the sources for his stories and explains different aspects of the stories. Look for songs and chants in his books.

Hutton, Warwick. Illustrator and reteller of folktales, including *The Trojan Horse* (McElderry, 1992) and *Odysseus and the Cyclops* (McElderry, 1995). His line drawings and watercolor washes are also found in picture books based on Bible stories.

Hyman, Trina Schart. Illustrator whose treatment of fairy tales typically includes a series of borders that enclose a page of text and a page of illustration. Examples of her detailed and realistic characters and settings can be seen in *Bearskin* by Howard Pyle (Morrow, 1997) and *King Stork* by Howard Pyle, reissued with new illustrations by Morrow, 1998.

Kellogg, Steven. Illustrator and author. His unrestrained, humorous style is well matched with his retelling of tall tales and folktales or his chaotic situations about "Pinkerton" based on his Great Dane. He typically uses watercolors, colored inks, and acrylics. Examples include his tall tale *Sally Ann Thunder Ann Whirlwind Crockett* (Morrow, 1995) and his fractured fairy tale, *The Three Little Pigs* (Morrow, 1997).

Kimmel, Eric. Storyteller of tales from around the world. Recents tales told by Kimmel include *The Tale of Ali Baba and the Forty Thieves: A Story from the Arabian Nights*, illustrated by Will Hillenbrand (Holiday House, 1996) and *One Eye, Two Eyes, Three Eyes: A Hutzul Tale*, illustrated by Dirk Zimmer (Holiday House, 1996).

Kraus, Robert. *Fables Aesop Never Wrote but Robert Kraus Did.* Viking, 1994.

Lattimore, Deborah Nourse, reteller and illustrator. *Arabian Nights: Three Tales.* HarperCollins, 1995.

Lester, Julius. Author of nonfiction, story collections, and folktales from the African-American tradition, including *John Henry*, illustrated by Jerry Pinkney (Dial, 1994).

McDermott, Gerald. Illustrator and author. McDermott blends modern art and folk design for a wide range of folklore. Examples include *Raven: A Trickster Tale from the Pacific Northwest* (Harcourt, 1993); *Coyote: A Trickster Tale from the American Southwest* (Harcourt, 1994) and *Musicians of the Sun* (Simon & Schuster, 1997).

Medearis, Angela Shelf. Adapter of West African folklore. *The Singing Man*, illustrated by Terea Shaffer (Holiday House, 1994), includes a pronunciation guide. *Tailypo: A Newfangled Tall Tale*, illustrated by Sterling Brown (Holiday House, 1996), is set in the United States.

Oughton, Jerrie. *The Magic Weaver of Rugs: A Tale of the Navajo*. Illustrated by Lisa Desimini. Houghton 1994.

Philip, Neil, reteller. *The Illustrated Book of Myths: Tales & Legends of the World*. Illustrated by Nilesh Mistry. Dorling Kindersley, 1995.

Pinkney, Jerry. Illustrator whose realistic African and African American characters are found in picture storybooks and folklore. *John Henry* by Julius Lester (Dial, 1994) provides one example of his ability to create a visual image that stays with the viewer. Another example is *The Sunday Outing* by Gloria Jean Pinkney (Dial, 1944).

Rockwell, Anne. Author and illustrator of bright color picture books, concept books, folklore, and information books. *The Robber Baby: Stories from the Greek Myths* (Greenwillow, 1994) has a pronunciation guide and acknowledgment of sources.

Sciezka, Jon. Author of parodies of folktales including *The True Story of the Three Little Pigs* (Viking, 1989) and *The Stinky Cheese Man & Other Fairly Stupid Tales* (Viking, 1992). Both books are illustrated by Lane Smith. This author/illustrator team also does the Time Warp Trio series of adventures for middle readers.

Shulevitz, Uri. Author and illustrator of folktales and fantasies (picture storybooks and chapter books) including Ehud Ben-Ezer's *Hosni the Dreamer: An Arabian Tale* (Farrar Straus Giroux, 1997). His *Writing with Pictures: How to Write and Illustrate Children's Books* (1985) is an excellent resource.

Smith, Lane. Illustrator of *The True Story of the Three Little Pigs* (Viking, 1989), and *The Stinky Cheese Man and Other Fairly Stupid Tales* (Viking, 1992). of *Math Curse* by Jon Sciezka (Viking, 1995) which combines drawings with collage creating modern abstract art. Others by this team include the Time Warp Trio series. See also Sciezka, Jon.

Stanley, Diane. See also information/biography section. *Rumpelstiltskin's Daughter* (Morrow, 1998).

Yep, Laurence. See also other sections for Yep. Yep is author of *The Junior Thunder Lord*, illustrated by Robert Van Nutt (Bridgewater, 1994) and *The Dragon Prince: A Chinese Beauty and the Beast Tale*, illustrated by Kam Mak (HarperCollins, 1997).

Young, Ed. Author and illustrator who uses a variety of media appropriate to the stories and folklore. His early years in China influence some of his works, while others reflect other cultures. Representative titles include *Lon Po Po: A Red*

Riding Hood Story from China (Philomel, 1989); *Night Visitors* (Philomel, 1995), *Moon Mother: A Native American Creation Story* (HarperCollins 1993); *Seven Blind Mice* (Philomel, 1992); and *Genesis* Adapted from the King James Version, A Laura Geringer Book (HarperCollins, 1997).

Zelinsky, Paul O. Illustrator and author of *Swamp Angel* by Anne Isaacs (Dutton, 1994) in which he used oil on cherry and maple veneers in an American Primitive style. In *Rapunzel* (Dutton, 1997) he is the reteller and describes the basis of his version and paints in the style of the old masters.

Chapter 9

Selecting Rhymes and Poetry

Three things are necessary for a writer
of children's poems: imagination, tech-
nique, and taste.

—James Reeves,
How to Write Poems for Children.

EXAMINING RHYMES AND POETRY

Poetry is the expression of ideas and feelings using words selected for their impression of sound, often arranged in rhythmic patterns. Poetry expresses thought and feeling with succinct, descriptive, evocative, exact, and carefully chosen words. **Rhymes** (nursery or Mother Goose), sidewalk jingles, greeting card verses, certain nonsense verses, and limericks are not considered poetry by some authorities. Others view poetry as a continuum balanced by doggerel at one end and lyrical poetry at the other end. There is agreement, however, that nursery rhymes and nonsense verses prepare the child for the appreciation of poetry.

MOTHER GOOSE AND OTHER RHYMES

Mother Goose rhymes and jingles appeal to children through ages four and five. They can serve as an introduction to the world of literature. Young children can hear rhyme, alliteration, and onomatopoeia in such verses. The sound patterns, simple stories with quick action, interesting characters, and humor, appeal to young children. Their brevity prepares children for longer and more involved verse. Other forms that appeal to young children include street cries, tongue twisters, counting rhymes, finger plays, and riddles.

Our traditional Mother Goose rhymes come from the English-speaking world. In Great Britain they are known as nursery rhymes. However, such rhymes are not peculiar to English-speaking cultures. All countries have rhymes and jingles that are appropriate for small children.

Special Criteria

You will have to decide which of these criteria are important for the specific work you are evaluating. For example: one book may feature well-known rhymes, while another will have newer rhymes. Both should be in the collection balancing old and new rhymes.

COVERAGE

- How many rhymes are included?
- Does the collection include both well-known and newer rhymes?
- Are the versions familiar ones?
- Does the text read smoothly?
- Are there different types of rhymes in the collection?
- Are the rhymes about one or more subjects or themes?
- Does the collection include rhymes from different countries?
- Are the rhymes presented in both English and the original language? Does the translation overcome the inherent difficulty of conveying the language and humor of rhymes?
- Is information about symbolic poetry, such as political nursery rhymes, provided for teachers?
- Are there lists of further readings for teachers?

ILLUSTRATIONS

- Has only one medium been used or several?
- Is the medium appropriate for the mood of the collection?
- Are the illustrations colorful?
- Is the style of the artwork appropriate for the collection?
- Do the illustrations complement or explain the text?
- Do the illustrations capture the mood and humor of the rhymes?
- Does the design of the title page capture the mood and coverage of the collection?
- Do the cover and endpapers add to the collection?

SETTING

- Is the setting one that children will comprehend?
- Is the setting appropriate for the rhymes?
- Does the setting contribute to the collection?

CHARACTERS

- Do the characters include both children and adults?
- Do the characters represent various ethnic backgrounds fairly and accurately?
- Does the personality of the characters match the rhymes?
- Are animals personified or are they realistically portrayed?

ARRANGEMENT

- How are text and illustrations arranged on the page?
- Is the text for each verse on a separate page or on facing pages?
- Is the page cluttered with several verses and related illustrations?
- Are unifying illustrations used for related verses?
- How can one tell where one rhyme ends and another begins?
- Does each verse have a title to help identify beginning and end?
- Is there unity to the collection, or does it appear to have all unrelated rhymes?

SPECIAL FEATURES

- Is there a table of contents?
- Does the index include entries for title, first line, and subject?
- Are the sources of the verses identified?
- Is the book designed for use with one child or with a group of children?

Trends in Mother Goose and Other Rhymes

A recent trend in publishing these collections is to base an entire book on one Mother Goose rhyme or on a limited number of rhymes with a single theme. Examples are *Little Robin Redbreast: A Mother Goose Rhyme*, illustrated by Shari Halpern, and *We Are All in the Dumps with Jack and Guy*, illustrated by Maurice Sendak. Another trend is the bilingual collections. An example for children in kindergarten through second grade is Nancy Abraham Hall and Jill Syverson-Stork's *Los pollitos dicen: Juegos, rimas y canciones infantiles de paises de habla hispaña/ The Baby Chicks Sing: Traditional Games, Nursery Rhymes, and Songs from Spanish-Speaking Countries*, illustrated by Kay Chorao. This collection includes the musical arrangements.

POETRY FOR CHILDREN

Children initially prefer **narrative poems**, poems that relate a particular event or episode or that tell a long tale. One of the most popular narrative poems is *The Night Before Christmas* by Clement Moore. Children also enjoy other forms of poems, such as limericks, haiku, free verse, and concrete poetry. In fact, children can enjoy **lyrical poetry**, in which the poet describes emotions and thoughts rather than telling a story. Short lyrics make a good introduction to lyrical poetry. These experiences can introduce the child to how poetry captures a moment, a feeling, or a scene. The title of Eve Merriam's poem, "It Doesn't Always Have to Rhyme," addresses a point that confuses children about the difference between prose and poetry.

The following section describes some of the forms of poetry commonly found in books for children, identifies a sampling of the poets who appeal to children, and discusses criteria for selecting individual poems and anthologies.

Elements of Poetry

What are the characteristics of poetry? Virginia Witucke's response is in Table 9–1. Look for these elements in poetry books for children. How do the poets use them? How does the poet speak to and establish rapport with the child?

How and what do these elements contribute to a poem? What techniques do poets use? If you want to go beyond the following discussion to learn more about these elements, you can consult the works in the References and Professional Resources listings at the end of this chapter and the general books on children's literature identified in Chapter 1.

1. Language
   Poets make conscious decisions about which words to use. They tend to work with a limited number of words to express an idea or feeling, and they choose these words for their rhythm, sound, and meaning. They also choose how to arrange the words to influence the rhythm, sound, effect, and meaning of the poem. The words may have **connotative** meanings, ones of association for the reader, or **denotative** meanings (that is, explicit). The poem provides the context for the meaning and a variety of figures of speech convey the meanings.

   The words in poetry tend to be arranged to create rhyme, combinations of sounds, and repetition of sound. When looking for the rhyme pattern, people tend to think immediately of **end rhyme**, where sounds at the end of the line agree. But poets may also arrange sound patterns with rhyming words within a line as well as the devices of assonance, alliteration, and consonance. **Assonance** is the pattern in which the same vowel sound is heard within a line or within a few lines. **Alliteration** is the repetition of the same consonant at the beginning of words, and **consonance** is the repetition of the final consonant sounds.

Table 9-1 What Is Poetry?
1. Language
2. Experience
3. Emotion and thought
4. Noticing
5. Sensation
6. Original
7. Compressed
8. Rhythm
9. Form
10. A whole
11. A communicator and an audience

Source: Virginia Witucke, *Poetry in the Elementary School* (Dubuque, Iowa: Wm. C. Brown, 1970): 15–28.

Sound patterns may be repeated sounds and combinations of sounds in the words. Poets choose words that appeal to the ear or words with sounds that add to the effect. The poet's words may be real or imaginary. The term **onomatopoeia** refers to words that imitate the name of an object or action or illustrate the word's meaning. Examples of onomatopoeia include buzz, hiss, clump, snuffle.

Poets also make extensive use of **metaphor** and **similes**, two forms of comparison. A simile is the more direct and specific form of comparison. When you see the words "like" or "as" in a poem, the author is using a simile to make the connection between the two words. If the poet uses a verb or noun without "like" or "as" to imply comparison, it is a metaphor. In this case the poet uses one idea or object as if it were another idea or object. A form of metaphor is **personification**. By giving human attributes to things, the poet brings them into the reader's life. **Hyperbole**, or extravagant exaggeration, appeals to children and also suggests meanings for the words.

2. Experience.
Poems deal with real or imagined experiences, and should be experiences the child can comprehend. A key question is always whether the poetry speaks to the child? Poetry *about* childhood is usually for nostalgic adults rather than for children. Anthologies may include poems written with the child in mind, or poems written for adults that the compiler thinks will appeal to children. When you read poetry aloud to children their responses will give you a sense of the poem's effect. Note their body language, facial expressions, and attention span.

3. Emotion and thought.
   Poems deal with feelings and thought. A poet writes not only to convey a specific emotional response, but also to elicit a given response.
4. Noticing.
   Poets express their insight and vision to increase the reader's observations and awareness. Because of this, poems can help the child see unexpected relationships.
5. Sensation.
   Poets use descriptive and narrative language so the reader or listener can imagine a particular sight, sound, touch, taste, or smell.
6. Original.
   The poet creates a unique statement written with sincerity and honesty. In learning about poetry, you will begin to distinguish the difference between trite and original works and between the creative and the superficial. The more successful poems provide the reader with new experiences, including emotional ones, and new insights.
7. Compressed.
   Poetry is compact. Each word is carefully chosen; one term can convey many meanings. Poets use figurative language to achieve this compression. By comparing or contrasting two objects, ideas, or feelings—explicitly or implicitly—the connotation of one word or phrase gives meaning to another. Metaphors and similes are commonly used to help make these connections.
8. Rhythm.
   The **rhythm** of the poem, whether the beat or regular cadence of the poem, may be metered or spontaneous and implies movement and events. When formalized into **meter**, the poem's pattern of rhythm consists of beats and stresses. Each line is made up of a given number of accented and unaccented syllables that appear in a set order.
9. Form.
   Form refers to how the poem is structured and put together. Poems may have certain shapes created by writing a specified number of lines. Sound patterns also can shape a poem, for example, which lines rhyme.

   Among the traditional poetry forms are poems with two or more verses divided by empty space, stanzas with verses repeating the same pattern, and patterns of a regular meter and rhyme scheme. Of course, not all poems fall within these traditional patterns. In children's literature one finds various forms including ballad, limerick, haiku, free verse, and concrete poetry. Children's poets, like Myra Cohn Livingston, use a variety of forms. In her *Poem-Making: Ways to Begin Writing Poetry*, Livingston describes the elements of poetry, gives examples, and encourages children to find the form that is comfortable for them to use.

   The **ballad** or **folkpoem**, one of the earlier forms of poetry, is part of our oral tradition. The early ballads were transmitted orally by minstrels. Among the traditional folk ballads that children will recognize are "John Henry," "I Ride Old Paint," and "Yankee Doodle." Literary ballads share the characteristics of the traditional folk ballad, but the author is known.

Characteristics: The ballad
- presents a simple narrative, usually relating a single episode;
- can be adopted for singing or giving the effect of a song;
- makes frequent use of dialogue;
- has marked rhythm and rhyme;
- uses a repeated refrain; and
- each stanza consists of four lines, with the second and fourth lines rhyming.

The **limerick** form, with the rhythm and sound adding to the humor is a popular form for children to imitate.

Characteristics: The limerick
- is usually a narrative;
- is light verse, often nonsensical (humorous), about people's actions, manners, and idiosyncrasies;
- consists of one-stanza with five lines: lines one, three, and five rhyme and are of the same length; lines two and four rhyme and are of the same length, but shorter than the other lines.

The **haiku** is of Japanese origin. Children are able to grasp the simplicity of the images, and older children can create their own.

Characteristics: Haiku are
- lyric, unrhymed poems;
- not restricted by rhyme patterns;
- poems of seventeen syllables arranged in three lines of five, seven, and five syllables;
- single, simple word pictures designed to evoke feeling relating to nature.

Free verse does not have a particular meter, and it may lack rhyme. The line lengths are often irregular.

Characteristics: Free verse
- lacks regular rhyme and meter;
- depends on rhythm or cadence for its poetic form;
- may look different from a traditional poem on the printed page, but when read aloud sounds like traditional poetry;
- is reflective writing;
- often treats abstract and philosophical subjects;
- may use a philosophical type set that suggests a rhythmical unit or cadence

In **concrete poetry** the meaning is carried out by shape of poem or where the poem appears, for example, in a poem about a skyscraper, the type can be set so the words are in the shape of a skyscraper. A poem about a seal that looks like a seal is another example. Also, the viewers' experiences affect their interpretations of the poem. For example, if a variety of words appear on different parts of a mobile, two viewers may see different combinations and find different meanings.

Characteristics: Concrete poetry

- merges visual, verbal, and auditory elements;
- may be presented through arrangement of words, letters, and punctuation marks;
- is usually written and printed in a shape that portrays subject.

10. A whole.

The poet strives to unite the words, ideas, moods, pictures, feelings, rhythm, and structure into a harmonious whole. The poem provides the context in which the rhythm, sound, and sense of the words interact to bring meaning.

11. A communicator and an audience.

The poet serves as communicator and needs the reaction of the reader or listener as an audience. The audience may recognize an experience or feeling, or the poet may stimulate new ideas or feelings. The poet can help the reader appreciate something new or, through the poem, stimulate creativity.

Special Criteria for Poetry

GENERAL GUIDELINES

Read the poems aloud. Poetry comes from our oral tradition, and so the most effective test of a poem is an oral rendition. Using this technique helps you understand the poet's use of language and rhythm, know the timing of the poem, and appreciate the voice dynamics needed to interpret the poem.

Choose collections that include both contemporary and older poems.

Select poems that relate to a child's experience, not those that patronize childhood or give a nostalgic view of childhood.

Look for high quality poems that show effective use of rhythm, honesty of feeling, careful use of language, and vivid imagery. Avoid overly rhythmic, singsongy poems and those that are supersentimental, saccharine, and use unnatural affects.

Select poems a child can understand, whether the subject is real or imagined. Avoid the too difficult or too simple poem.

Avoid poems with obsolete or difficult language.

Look for fresh, original, unique poems. Avoid cliche burdened, hackneyed, merely "cute," preachy, and didactic works.

Select poets who respect the child as a person. Avoid the poet who is condescending or oversimplifies.

Look for poems of a length that appeals to children. Avoid long descriptive passages.

Look for poems of interest to children. Avoid ones that are pedantic or about a subject in which children have little interest.

Study poems, such as those by John Ciardi, that have stood the test of time to give yourself a "feel" for what is good.

THE SINGLE POEM, CRITERIA FOR SELECTING

GENERAL

- Is the poem unique?
- What is the purpose of the poem?
- Is the purpose appropriate for children?
- Does the poem appeal to children?
- How has the poet created the emotional intensity of the poem?

LANGUAGE

- Does the rhythm reinforce and create meaning for the poem?
- Is the rhyme natural sounding or contrived?
- Does the sound add meaning to the poem?
- Will a child understand the similes and metaphors?
- Does the poem create sensory images of sight, touch, sound, smell, and taste?
- What is the quality of the imagination in the poem?
- Will the child see something in a new way?

SHAPE

- Does the shape of the poem contribute to the meaning of the poem?
- Does the arrangement of the words contribute to the meaning of the poem?

ANTHOLOGIES, CRITERIA FOR SELECTING

PURPOSE

- What is the purpose of the collection?
- Is the purpose stated in the introduction or an opening section of the book?
- Does the purpose fill a need in the collection?
- Does the selection of poems included meet the purpose of the collection?
- Who is the intended audience?
- Are the selections appropriate for that audience?

SCOPE

- Are the poems by a variety of authors, familiar and unknown, traditional and contemporary?
- How many poems are included?
- Are the poems in other books in the collection?
- Do the poems relate to each other?
- Does the anthology include a variety of forms of poetry?

LANGUAGE

- Is there variety of meter found in the poems?
- Is there a variety of sound patterns in the poems? Do the poems include uses of alliteration, onomatopoeia, or repetition?
- Do the verse patterns enrich the content of the poems?
- Is figurative language imaginative and appropriate?

SUBJECTS

- Does the anthology focus on one subject?
- Will there be sufficient use of poems on that subject to merit purchasing it?
- Will the subject matter appeal to children?

ORGANIZATION

- How are the poems arranged and organized?
- Is there a table of contents?
- Are there one or more indexes?
- Can a reader locate poems by title, poet, first line, or subject?

ILLUSTRATIONS

- Do the illustrations enrich the poetry?
- Are the illustrations merely decorative?
- Are the illustrations placed appropriately?
- Do the illustrations distract from the poetry?

OTHER FEATURES

- Are there commentaries with background information about the poems?
- Is the source of each poem identified?
- Does the anthology include biographical information about each poet?
- Do the acknowledgments and copyright information sections provide more information about the poems?

Table 9.2 National Council of Teachers of English Excellence in Poetry for Children Award	
1977	David McCord
1978	Aileen Fisher
1979	Karla Kuskin
1980	Myra Cohn Livingston
1981	Eve Merriam
1982	John Ciardi
1985	Lillian Moore
1988	Arnold Adoff
1991	Valerie Worth
1994	Barbara Esbensen
1997	Eloise Greenfield

PHYSICAL BOOK

- Is the paper of appropriate quality?
- Is the paper an appropriate color for the subject or mood of the poetry?
- Is the page layout uncluttered?
- Is the size of the book one a child can handle?
- Is the size of print appropriate for the intended audience?
- Do white spaces or frames set off individual poems?

Poetry Awards as Guides: Excellence in Poetry for Children Award

If you are not familiar with authors of children's poetry, you can begin with the works by poets who received the National Council of Teachers of English Excellence in Poetry for Children Award. This award recognizes a poet's entire body of poetry written for children ages 3 through 13, not a particular poem or book of poetry.

The award began in 1977, was awarded annually until 1982, and now is awarded every three years.

A poet who did not receive this particular award, but one to look for, is Deborah Chandra, author of *Balloons and Other Poems*. She is the first recipient of the International Reading Association's Lee Bennett Hopkins Promising Poet Award. This award, first presented in 1995, will be given every three years to a new author of children's poetry. It is named for Lee Bennett Hopkins, who is well known for his poetry and for his success as a compiler of anthologies. Other poets are listed at the end of the chapter.

To locate poems, check the *Index to Poetry for Children and Young People: 1993–1997*, compiled by G. Meredith Blackburn, III. The index lists title, author, subject, and first line for nearly 8,000 poems in 123 anthologies.

SUMMARY

Poets express their ideas and feelings in a variety of forms, from traditional poems like the ballad to free verse or concrete poetry. The characteristics of the form and whether the poem is published alone in a single book or with others in an anthology lead to the criteria used in evaluating poetry.

TITLES MENTIONED IN THIS CHAPTER

Balloons and Other Poems by Deborah Chandra. Farrar, Straus & Giroux, 1993.

Index to Poetry for Children and Young People, 1993–1997: A Title, Subject, Author, and First Line Index to Poetry in Collections for Children and Young People. Blackburn, G. Meredith, III, compiler. Wilson, 1998.

Little Robin Redbreast: A Mother Goose Rhyme, by Shari Halpern. North South, 1994.

Los pollitos dicen: Juegos, rimas y canciones infantiles de paises de habla hispaña/ The Baby Chicks Sing: Traditional Games, Nursery Rhymes, and Songs from Spanish-Speaking Countries, by Nancy Abraham Hall and Jill Syverson-Stork, illustrated by Kay Chorao. Little, Brown, 1994.

Poem-Making: Ways to Begin Writing Poetry by Myra Cohn Livingston. HarperCollins, 1991.

We Are All in the Dumps with Jack and Guy illustrated by Maurice Sendak. HarperCollins, 1993.

REFERENCES

Livingstone, Dinah. 1993. *Poetry Handbook for Readers and Writers.* London: Macmillan.

Reeves, James. 1971. *How to Write Poems for Children.* London, Heinemann.

Witucke, Virginia. 1970. *Poetry in the Elementary School.* Pose Lamb, consulting editor. Literature for Children series. Dubuque, Ia.: Wm. C. Brown Company.

RECOMMENDED PROFESSIONAL RESOURCES

Livingston, Myra Cohn. 1990. *Climb into the Bell Tower: Essays on Poetry.* New York: Harper and Row.

    Discusses characteristics of quality poetry and pays tribute to the contributions of Edward Lear, David McCord, Harry Behn, John Ciardi, Norma Farber, Randall Jarrell, X. J. Kennedy, Eve Merriam, Jack Prelutsky, Shel Silverstein, and Valerie Worth.

————. *Poem-Making: Ways to Begin Writing Poetry.* 1991. HarperCollins.

    Although written for children, adults will find this a useful guide to learning about the elements of poetry and how to differentiate the "good" from "poor."

McElmeel, Sharon L. 1993. *The Poet Tree*. Englewood, Colo.: Teacher Ideas Press.

Provides biographical information about poets with ideas for activities and curriculum connections. Defines poetry terms.

Steinbergh, Judith Wolinsky. 1994. *Reading and Writing Poetry: A Guide for Teachers, Grades K-4*. New York: Scholastic Professional Books.

The author, a poet, describes activities and techniques to use with children as they learn to listen to poetry. Covers playing with forms: acrostics, haiku, cinquain, pantoum, playground chants, cheers, blues, and rope chants.

REPRESENTATIVE POETS BY FORM

Poets of limericks
Edward Lear
John Ciardi
Ogden Nash
Jack Prelutsky
X. J. Kennedy

Haiku poets
Harry Behn
Richard Lewis
Doris Johnson
Easho
Issa
Joso
Kazue Mizumura

Free verse poets
William Jay Smith
Ann Clark
Dorothy Baruch
Hilda Conkling
Carl Sandburg
Langston Hughes
Marianne Moore
Mary Neville
Aliki Barnstone
Valerie Worth

Concrete Poets
Robert Froman, "Skyscratcher"
Myra Cohn Livingston, "Buildings"

REPRESENTATIVE POETS AND COMPILERS

Adoff, Arnold. Poet and anthologist. His *Love Letters*, illustrated by Lisa Desimini (Blue Sky Press, 1997) is in the tradition of giving valentines.

Bierhorst, John, selector. *On the Road of Stars: Native American Night Poems and Sleep Charms*, illustrated by Judy Pedersen (Macmillan, 1994) has an author's note and a list of sources.

Bryan, Ashley. Author, illustrator, and story teller who uses poetry to tell the story. He celebrates life from an African-American perspective. One example is *Sing to the Sun*, HarperCollins, 1992. In *Ashley Bryan's ABC of African American Poetry* (Atheneum, 1997) he chooses a line from the poem that inspired the illustrations. *Ashley Bryan's African Tales, Uh-Huh* (Atheneum, 1998) has examples of his appealing abilities as a reteller and illustrator.

Cole, Joanna, and Stephanie Calmenson. *Yours Till Banana Splits: 201 Autograph Rhymes*, illustrated by Alan Tiegreen (Morrow, 1995) opens up another way to get children to think about rhymes.

Esbensen, Barbara Juster. Poet. *Dance With Me*, illustrated by Megan Lloyd (HarperCollins, 1995), is a celebration of dance whether by people or through nature with a breeze blowing flowers. *Echoes for the Eye: Poems to Celebrate Patterns in Nature*, illustrated by Helen K. Davie (HarperCollins, 1996), leads the listener to look for spirals, branches, polygons, meanders, and circles.

Florian, Douglas. Author and illustrator. His *Beast Feast* (Harcourt Brace, 1994) is typical with its humor in both the poetry and the watercolor paintings. Other titles are *In the Swim: Poems and Paintings* (Harcourt Brace, 1997) and *Insectlopedia: Poems & Paintings* (Harcourt Brace, 1998).

Greenfield, Eloise. Poet and author who portrays strong African-American people in her works that express the joy of living. One example is *For the Love of the Game: Michael Jordan and Me* illustrated by Jan Spivey Gilchrist (HarperCollins, 1997).

Hopkins, Lee Bennett. Poet and anthologist. *Good Rhymes and Good Times* (HarperCollins, 1995) captures everyday experiences children share regardless of color. Compiles anthologies for young readers, such as *Weather* (An I Can Read Book; HarperCollins, 1994). Another anthology *Marvelous Math: A Book of Poems*, illustrated by Karen Barbour (Simon & Schuster, 1997) reminds us that mathematics is in our daily lives.

Lear, Edward. Two examples that capture his humor are *There Was an Old Man: A Gallery of Nonsense Rhymes*, illustrated by Michele Lemieux (Morrow 1994), and *The Pelican Chorus and Other Nonsense*, illustrated by Fred Marcellino (HarperCollins, 1995).

Lewis, J. Patrick. Poet. His *Black Swan, White Crow*, with woodcuts by Chris Manson (Atheneum, 1995), includes author's note about haiku and suggests that the reader try writing some. *Doodle Dandies: Poems That Take Shape* (Atheneum, 1998) with illustrations by Lisa Desimini can be used to involve readers in deciphering the shapes.

Mado, Michio. Internationally known author of poems and songs. *The Magic Pocket* (McElderry, 1998) was translated by The Empress Michiko of Japan and the illustrations are by Mitsumasa Anno. Includes the Japanese and English text for each poem.

Nye, Naomi Shihab. Selector. *The Tree Is Older Than You Are: A Bilingual Gathering of Poems and Stories from Mexico with Paintings by Mexican Artists* (Simon and Schuster, 1995). Includes text first in Spanish and then in English. Provides an introduction to the artistic efforts of poets and artists for intermediate grade students.

Prelutsky, Jack. Writer and anthologist associated with humorous verses. Both *The Dragons are Singing Tonight* (Greenwillow 1993) and *Monday's Troll* (Greenwillow, 1996) are illustrated by Peter Sís. His anthology *A Pizza the Size of the Sun* is illustrated by James Stevenson (Greenwillow, 1996). Prelutsky's well-received *Random House Book of Poetry for Children: A Treasury of 572 Poems for Today's Child*, illustrated by Arnold Lobel (Random House, 1983), is still in print as of this writing.

Silverstein, Shel. Poet, author, songwriter, and illustrator known for his humorous poetry and drawings. His poems range from the silly to the serious, deal with anything from philosophical issues to ridiculous topics, and reflect the fears and dreams of children. An example is *Falling Up* (IIarperCollins, 1996).

Stevenson, James. Illustrator, poet, and author. Three examples of his poetic works are *Popcorn* (Greenwillow, 1998), *Sweet Corn* (Greenwillow, 1995), and *Candy Corn* (Greenwillow, 1999).

Wong, Janet S. Poet. She draws on her Korean, Chinese, and American background and observes the differences between their customs and cultures. See *A Suitcase of Seaweed and Other Poems* (McElderry, 1996) and *Good Luck Gold and Other Poems* (McElderry, 1994).

Chapter 10

Selecting Information Books

> *A child uses information books to assemble what he knows, what he feels, what he sees, as well as to collect new facts. His reaction to something as ordinary as a loaf [of bread] may be, at one time or another, one of wonder, excitement, interest, aesthetic pleasure, physical satisfaction, curiosity.*
> —Margery Fisher, *Matters of Fact: Aspects of Non-fiction for Children.*

EXAMINING INFORMATION BOOKS

Information books are written to inform, to lead the child from a fact or facts to a concept or a principle. The author's attitude (tone) toward subject and reader affects the reception of fact and concept. The author writing information books for children faces the challenge of children's lack of experience. The task is to arouse their curiosity without suggesting that the facts are miraculous or beyond their comprehension. The ultimate goal is to lead the child to discovery that may extend into their adult lives.

Information seekers in an elementary school represent a wide range of ages, possibly preschoolers through professional personnel. Alphabet books, counting books, and simple concept books often found in the "Easy" section can provide

Orbis Pictus by Amos Comenius, published in 1657, is recognized as the first known nonfiction book for children. Woodcuts illustrated everyday objects.

information for the younger children. Older children doing research reports will seek books with footnotes and other forms of documentation for the author's sources. Staff and professional personnel will use a wide range of information titles on education-related subjects housed in the professional collection.

Just as the range of ages is wide, so are the topics. They may be natural science identification books or explorations of complex subjects such as democracy. Topics commonly found in elementary school collections reflect the wide range of subjects in the curriculum and the interests of children.

To set the stage for thinking about criteria for selecting information books, consider commonly accepted desirable characteristics of such titles. Key words describing desirable characteristics include accuracy, engaging style, clear writing, and logically developed information. The writer's integrity is important. Authors should be honest with their readers by identifying their points of view, sharing their interest in the subject, and encouraging questioning attitudes on the reader's part. Representative titles are listed at the end of this chapter.

In addition to the general criteria described in this chapter, there are characteristics unique to various subjects. The next chapter will discuss those characteristics and identify appropriate questions to consider in selecting such books.

AWARD BOOKS AS GUIDES: *ORBIS PICTUS* AWARD

Examples of well-written information books are those that have received the National Council of Teachers of English's *Orbis Pictus* Award for Outstanding Nonfiction. Established in 1989, the award is to recognize and promote excellence in nonfiction writing for children. The committee's decision is based on accuracy, content, style, organization, illustration, and format.

COMPONENTS OF INFORMATION BOOKS

Authors work with elements of intellectual content when writing information books. They determine the scope of the book, do research for accuracy of information, and decide how they want to treat their subject. One of the important decisions they make is how they will organize the information. They are concerned, as are all writers, with the use of language. In information books special features such as indexes, glossaries, and appendices may be prime sources of information. Maps, charts, and photographs may be key visual sources of information. Like other writers, good authors of information books are cognizant of our diverse society and the ability levels of young readers.

Table 10-1 *Orbis Pictus* Award for Outstanding Nonfiction Sponsored by the National Council of Teachers of English			
1990	*The Great Little Madison*	Jean Fritz	Putnam, 1989
1991	*Franklin Delano Roosevelt*	Russell Freedman	Clarion, 1990
1992	*Flight: The Story of Charles Lindbergh*	Robert Burleigh	Philomel, 1991
1993	*Children of the Dust Bowl: The True Story of the School at Weedpatch Camp*	Jerry Stanley	Crown, 1992
1994	*Across America on an Immigrant Train*	Jim Murphy	Clarion, 1993
1995	*Safari Beneath the Sea: The Wonder World of the North Pacific Coast*	Diane Swanson	Sierra Club Books, 1994
1996	The Great Fire	Jim Murphy	Scholastic, 1995
1997	*Leonardo da Vinci*	Diane Stanley	Morrow, 1996
1998	*An Extraordinary Life: The Story of a Monarch Butterfly*	Laurence Pringle	Orchard, 1997

CRITERIA AND GUIDELINES FOR COMPONENTS OF INFORMATION BOOKS

Scope

A challenge for writers of informational books is how to focus and when to quit. The writer must chose a key idea, relate it to facts and concepts that are familiar to the child, clarify the concept, and then lead the child to becoming a future problem solver.

CRITERIA

Questions to consider:
- Are all significant facts included?
- Is the subject adequately covered?
- Is there sufficient content to make the book informative?
- Does the book provide enough information to merit its purchase?
- In books for young readers is the author able to limit the scope of the subject while retaining important facts and presenting them logically?

Accuracy

Information is always changing regardless of the subject. Recent discoveries, for instance, have revealed new information about planets and dinosaurs. In the field of technology changes occur rapidly. Political boundaries change and countries are renamed. The author is challenged to provide up-to-date information, current proper spelling of words, and clear explanations of theories, while identifying opinions and biases.

CRITERIA

Questions that address these points:

- Are facts, theories, and opinions clearly distinguished?
- Is the copyright date recent? If this version of the book is a revision, has material been updated where needed?
- Does the author document the original source of the information or illustrations where appropriate? Citations can be found in footnotes, source notes for photographs and other graphic materials, an author's note, a bibliography, or in a section entitled "Acknowledgements".
- Does the author acknowledge the help of a subject specialist in checking the book for accuracy?
- Do the facts differ from ones found in other books or reference materials?
- In historical and biographical works does interpretation of persons and events reflect current scholarship?
- Is the setting accurate in terms of time period, geographic location, social and political order, speech patterns, and costume?

Treatment

Traditionally books classified with a Dewey Decimal number and shelved in the section of the library labeled **nonfiction** were considered the information books: those written to present and discuss facts. Today, students will also find **blended books**, which Gloria Shurzynski describes as being "half fiction and half nonfiction" (Shurzynski, 1992:46). Well-known examples are David Macaulay's *Cathedral* and Joanna Cole's Magic School Bus series. Fictionalized biographies provide another example of mixing facts and fiction. To select these books one must apply criteria used for the more traditional nonfiction works as well as the criteria for fiction. The emphasis in this chapter will be on criteria for the informational aspects of these books.

In writing either nonfiction or blended books, authors need to go beyond the minimal presentation of facts. They should help the child ask questions while stimulating the child's imagination and interest. Writers can alert readers to potential for new discoveries by using phrases such as "scientists believe," "so far as we know," "perhaps," and "may have." They also can point out that the young reader could have an opportunity to contribute to the expansion of this knowledge in the future.

Writers can broaden the child's perspective by putting the topic in a broader context and pointing out relationships instead of limiting the discussion to bare facts. For example, an event can be described in the context of the historical period. Relationships can be drawn between the event and its integration into the arts, architecture, myths, folklore, botany, biography, music, science, and crafts of that time period. A writer of biographical works can create a social history by creating a sense of the people and the times.

CRITERIA

Questions to consider:

- Is the level of knowledge needed to use or understand the material in the book appropriate for the intended audience?
- In historical works are important preceding and subsequent events presented?
- Does the author create dramatic moments without resorting to cliches?
- Are statistics used judiciously without bombarding the reader?
- Are facts presented in a context meaningful to the child?
- Are facts provided and used to support generalizations?
- Are scientific terms and concepts presented clearly and defined within a context familiar to the child?
- When the author states a personal opinion or offers an interpretation is there evidence to support the author's statement?
- Does the book include different viewpoints on a subject?
- Does the book encourage the reader to inquire further about the subject?
- Does the book show the context and relationships of the topic?
- Does the book discuss the broader picture such as social issues?
- Does the book use problem-solving situations that include open-ended questions, models for observation, and suggestions for further exploration?
- Do the illustrations and text encourage the child to reflect on a topic, rather than jump from one topic to another?
- If social life and customs are being discussed, does the author demonstrate respect for ethnicity and plurality?

Organization of Information

The method by which the author organizes and presents information can help or hinder the reader's use of the books. Linda DeGroff (DeGroff, 1990:496) identifies common patterns by which writers organize information:

1. Alphabetical
2. Order of interest to the author or reader
3. Chronological
4. Place and spatial relations
5. Cause and effect
6. Uses
7. Comparison
8. Discovery or invention
9. Degree of familiarity
10. Classified or subject (broad) to sub-subjects (narrow)

Each pattern has advantages and disadvantages for the reader. In an alphabetical arrangement the reader must use the same term as the author. The "order of interest," an attention getter, may be of low information value. The chronological approach is appropriate for a) history of a country, a culture, or a region, b) history of a family or person, or c) life cycles of animals. However, young readers may lack the sense of time needed to understand chronological relationships. A chronology can be used in context of a journal for one day or a specific time period, as in *Stranded at Plimouth Plantation, 1626*.

Place and spatial relations are commonly used in geographic information. The cause and effect approach may be too complex for the child's ability, although the author may want the reader to discover the connection. "Use," a practical approach, may group unrelated facts together. Comparisons are commonly found in dictionaries with the groupings of synonyms and antonyms of a word. Other examples of comparisons include comparing similarities and differences of wild and tame animals or comparing traditional and contemporary social practices.

Basing a biography on a single discovery or invention may tend to shove the scientific problems and facts around and create a one-sided picture of the subject. Books for younger children may move from the familiar to the unknown with the emphasis on the facts as separate pieces of information. An example of the classified or broad subject to sub-subjects approach is moving from storms to types of storms, such as thunderstorms, hailstorms, and snowstorms.

CRITERIA

Questions to consider:

- Is the information presented in a logical order?
- Is the system of organization appropriate for the subject, purpose of the book, and the intended audience?
- Do headings and subheadings help to access a topic?

LITERARY MERIT

Like writers of other genres, the authors of information books are concerned with style or how they use language. Here are some desirable characteristics.

- simple and effective comparisons
- variety in sentence length and construction
- use of imagery and figurative language

CRITERIA

Questions to consider:

- Is the book clearly written?
- Are ideas logically developed?
- Will the text catch and hold the interest of the reader?
- Will the book be a good "read aloud"?
- Is there a central issue or problem?
- Is there a theme or main idea?
- Is there a sequence of events or an account of accurate and current factual evidence that clarifies or offers solutions to a problem?
- Is there a point of view or narrative voice?
- Does the writing have a distinctive tone?

Special Features

Access to information is another critical factor. Tables of contents, indexes, and the change of type size for different sections can help the reader locate specific information. In fact, a 64-page book can benefit from an index because of the large number of facts that are frequently found even in this size book.

CRITERIA

Questions to consider:

- Does the book provide access to the information through a table of contents; lists of tables, charts, and illustrations; the use of headings and subheadings within the text; indexes; or a glossary with guides to pronunciation?
- Does the index have cross references?
- Does the book lead the reader to further information with appendices, bibliographies for further reading, or suggested activities?

Illustrative Materials

Information may be presented solely through text; through a combination of text and illustrations as in **photoessays**, where both play important roles; or through illustrations that provide information not repeated in the text. Each approach calls for appropriate assessment. Visual materials can provide a means for less able to reluctant readers to obtain information and should be evaluated for that potential use.

CRITERIA

Questions to consider:

- Do the illustrations clarify the text?
- Are illustrative materials captioned?
- Are diagrams, drawings, and maps clearly labeled?
- Is distortion avoided in charts and graphs?
- Are relative sizes shown?
- Are drawings and photographs sharp and clear?
- Are enlargements or other magnifications labeled?
- Are the illustrations positioned close to the appropriate text?
- Do the illustrations add aesthetic appeal to the book?
- Are the sources cited?
- In activity books are children pictured doing age-appropriate activities with adults shown performing the more dangerous procedures?
- Does the **legend**, or the explanation accompanying photographs or other illustrative material, repeat information in the text or provide additional information? Look at Jim Murphy's *The Great Fire* to see how the legends can supplement and support the text. Notice, too, how the map is used throughout the book to illustrate the spreading of the fire. You also will find source notes acknowledging the original source of the illustrations.
- What role do illustrations play in the presentation of information?
- Are different type fonts used to indicate new subjects or different levels of information?

Multicultural Aspects

This is a good time to go back and review the American Association for the Advancement of Science's "Equity Guidelines" presented in the criteria for multicultural literature in Chapter 4.

Buyer Beware!
Avoid these undesirable elements: • Condescension (talking down to the reader) • Oversimplification (simplifying information so that it is distorted) • Anthropomorphism (assigning human behavior to animals) • Didacticism (preaching) • Propaganda (generalizations without factual support) • Confusing information • Sloppy writing • Inaccuracy • Lack of respect for the subject

CRITERIA AND GUIDELINES FOR TYPES OF INFORMATION BOOKS

Series

A large number of nonfiction series exist. One example is the British-based Dorling Kindersley "Eyewitness Books" which have close-up photographs on white paper with clear labels and eye-catching designs. These books are physically appealing. As you consider them, think about the amount of information provided. Do the visuals present sufficient information to help your students? Does the text also provide information? Which books already in the collection will complement these when students are preparing reports?

Series to avoid are those with pedantic writing, use of unfamiliar terms and concepts, limited information, and unappealing format. These are often formula books with a format that may not permit full inclusion of appropriate information.

CRITERIA

As with series in other genres, there are questions one should consider before selecting these titles.

- Are there inconsistencies within a series?
- Are there inconsistencies between different series published by the same company?
- If the series originally was published in another country, will U.S. children understand the language and concepts used in the presentation?
- Is there sufficient information to make the book worth purchasing?
- Is the research, enthusiasm for the subject, and depth of coverage equal to that found in other titles?

Concept Books

Concept books are designed to introduce young children to shapes, colors, sizes, a class of objects, or an abstract idea. The information may consist of photographs or other illustrations with no words or labeled images of the object. Tana Hoban's *So Many Circles, So Many Squares* (Greenwillow, 1998) and *Look Book* (Greenwillow, 1997) are two examples of how a skilled photographer can present information. Concept books usually do not have story lines.

CRITERIA

Questions to consider in evaluating concept books:

- Is a provocative concept introduced?
- Does the book help the child see similarities and differences?
- Does the book help the child see relationships?
- Does the book help a child develop a vocabulary?
- Is the object or the class of objects clear?
- Are the functions of the objects clear?
- Does the information move from familiar to unfamiliar?
- Does the information move from simple to complex?

Alphabet Books

Alphabet books have different purposes and uses. A common purpose is to teach the name and shape of letters to young children through a word and picture; sometimes there is a narrative. More advanced presentations involve the use of riddles or puzzles and engage the child in hunting for hidden pictures, locating obscure objects, and noting the positioning of letters. Other characteristics that add appeal are the use of alliteration and a rhyming text. For alphabet books that use unfamiliar objects, such as birds or herbs, a glossary is helpful.

The alphabet also may be used to organize information about a subject or theme. Titles, such as *V is for Vanishing: An Alphabet of Endangered Animals,* are often shelved with other nonfiction works. Some alphabet books turn out to be showcases for artwork rather than vehicles for accurate teaching of the alphabet.

For social studies units Lisa Nicklow notes that alphabet books such as *Ashanti to Zulu: African Traditions* can be used to introduce students to new concepts and ideas at the beginning of a unit of study, to review main ideas when concluding a unit, or to initiate group discussions or creative activities such as drama, art, or written expression (Nicklow, 1995: 3).

CRITERIA

Criteria for books designed to teach the name and shape of letters:

- What is the real purpose of the book?
- Who is the intended audience?
- Are the objects or animals clearly presented?
- Will the child recognize the objects or animals?
- Does the author or illustrator avoid using an object that may be known by several names?
- Are upper- and lowercase letters used appropriately?
- Where is the letter placed in relation to the object or animals that illustrate it?
- Is each letter fully formed?
- Is the style of print appropriate for the audience?
- Are the words used appropriate for the audience?
- Does the organization and development of the material create a unified book?

SUMMARY

The components of information books—scope, accuracy, treatment, organization of information, literary merit, special features, illustrative materials, and multicultural aspects—serve as points on which criteria can be established for judging individual books. Books in series, concept books, and alphabet books raise additional questions to consider when making selection decisions.

TITLES MENTIONED IN THIS CHAPTER

Ashanti to Zulu: African Traditions by Margaret Musgrove, illustrated by Leo and Diane Dillon. Dial, 1976.

Cathedral: The Story of Its Construction by David Macaulay. Houghton Mifflin, 1973.

Eyewitness Books series by Dorling Kindersley.

The Great Fire by Jim Murphy. Scholastic, 1995.

Look Book by Tana Hoban. Greenwillow, 1997.

Magic School Bus series by Joanna Cole. Two titles are *The Magic School Bus in the Time of the Dinosaurs* (Scholastic 1995) and *The Magic School Bus Plays Ball: A Book about Forces* (Scholastic 1998).

So Many Circles, So Many Squares by Tana Hoban. Greenwillow, 1998.

Stranded at Plimouth Plantation 1626 by Gary Bowen. HarperCollins, 1994.

V is for Vanishing: An Alphabet of Endangered Animals by Patricia Mullins. HarperCollins, 1994.

REFERENCES

American Association for the Advancement of Science. 1995. "Equity Guidelines." *Science Books and Films* 31, no.3 (April): 65–67, 90.

DeGroff, Linda. 1990. "Information Books: Topics and Structures." *The Reading Teacher* 43, no. 7 (March): 496–501.

Fisher, Margery. 1972. *Matters of Fact: Aspects of Non-fiction for Children*. New York: Crowell.

Fritz, Jean. Nd. "Partners in the Quest for Truth" *The Basics of Writing for Children and Young Adults* A Writer's Digest Guide, 11: 66–68, 70.

Gath, Tracy. 1995. "Science Books & Films Celebrate 30 Years." *Science Books & Films* 31, no. 3 (April): 65–67, 90.

Manning, Pat, and Alan R. Newman. 1986. "Safety Isn't Always First: A Disturbing Look at Chemistry Books." *School Library Journal* 33, no. 2 (October): 99–102.

Nicklow, Lisa. 1995. "Integrating Literature into the Social Studies Curriculum: Alphabet Books—The Forgotten Genre." *Social Studies and the Young Learner* 7, no. 2 (November/December): 1–4.

Shurzynski, Gloria. 1992. "Blended Books." *School Library Journal* 38, no. 10 (October): 46–47.

RECOMMENDED PROFESSIONAL RESOURCES

Arnold, Caroline. 1998. "Writing a Photo-Essay" in "The Inside Story" column, *Book Links* 7, no. 5 (May): 56–58.

Arnold's perspective on writing this type of information book.

McElmeel, Sharon L. *Great New Nonfiction Reads*. Englewood, Colo.: Libraries Unlimited, 1995.

Identifies 620 titles for reading aloud or sharing with young readers. Discusses how to connect poetry, folklore, fairy tales, songs, and fiction to information. Provides bibliographic information; ISBN; Dewey Classification and Cutter number; target audience: grades, age; descriptive annotation; and related titles with annotations. Indexes by author, title, illustrator, and subject.

ALPHABET BOOKS

ABC Book by C. B. Falls. Morrow, 1998.

Reissue of this woodblock illustrated classic.

Action Alphabet by Shelley Rotner. Atheneum, 1996.

Full color photographs of culturally diverse children engaged in physical activities.

Alphabet City by Stephen T. Johnson. Viking, 1995.

An example of an alphabet book for older children and adults. The photographic appearance of these illustrations in this Caldecott Honor book is misleading. Pastels, watercolors, gouache, and charcoal were used on hot pressed watercolor paper to create the images.

The Alphabet from Z to A (With Much Confusion on the Way) by Judith Viorst, illustrated by Richard Hull. Atheneum, 1994.

An interactive book of poetry designed for older children who understand the vagaries of spelling.

The Alphabet Tale by Jan Garten, illustrated by Muriel Batherman. Greenwillow, 1994.

This rhyming interactive book is designed for younger children. The tail on the cover of the book leads across the endpages, throughout the book, and to the back cover.

Ashley Bryan's ABC of African American Poetry by Ashley Bryan. Atheneum, 1997.

Colorful tempera and gouache paintings provide the visual images for poems or fragments of poems by African Americans.

Caribbean Alphabet by Frané Lessac. Tambourine, 1994.

Gouache primitive paintings introduce children to the Caribbean culture. Unfamiliar terms are defined in the glossary.

C is for City by Nikki Grimes and Pat Cummings. Lothrop, Lee & Shepard, 1995.

Within the rhyming verse and the illustrations, the reader's attention is drawn to city life.

An Edible Alphabet by Bonnie Christensen. Dial, 1994.

Illustrated with wood engravings, this book provides a glossary that identifies the plants.

The Graphic Alphabet by David Pelletier. Orchard, 1996.

This Caldecott Honor book is a visual experience with its computer-generated illustrations.

The Handmade Alphabet by Laura Rankin. Dial, 1991.

Rankin provides a colorful introduction to the alphabet and to signing.

Handsigns, A Sign Language Alphabet by Kathleen Fain. Chronicle, 1993.

Another introduction to signing the alphabet.

The Hullabaloo ABC by Beverly Cleary, illustrated by Ted Rand. Morrow, 1998.

Realistic watercolor illustrations depict three children's activities on a farm.

A Jewish Holiday ABC by Malka Drucker, illustrated by Rita Pocock. Harcourt, 1992.

This alphabet introduces the reader to ten holidays.

REPRESENTATIVE AUTHORS AND ILLUSTRATORS

Note: Additional authors are identified at the end of the next chapter.

Ancona, George. Photographer who is skilled in selecting and framing his photographs. His photoessays have full-color detailed photographs. Representative works include *Earth Daughter: Alicia of Acoma Pueblo* (Simon & Schuster,

1995), a bilingual book, *The Piñata Maker: El Piñatero.*(Harcourt,1994), and *Let's Dance!* (Morrow, 1998).

Arnosky, Jim. Realistic illustrator, naturalist, and artist. Representative titles include *All Night Near the Water* (Putnam, 1994), *Rabbits and Raindrops* (Putnum, 1997), and *All about Owls* (Scholastic, 1995). His imaginary character Crinkleroot is found leading the reader to information in a number of guide books published by Simon & Schuster.

Calmenson, Stephanie, see Cole, Joanna.

Cole, Joanna. Author of the popular Magic School Bus series (illustrated by Bruce Degen), who combines facts and humor into informational books. For younger children she presents information with photoessays (*How You Were Born,* Morrow, 1993, and *The New Baby at Your House*, Morrow, 1998; both are photographed by Margaret Miller). With Stephanie Calmenson she has authored a number of activity books involving card games, beginning to read skills, and collecting autograph sayings.

Degen, Bruce, see Cole, Joanna.

Fisher, Leonard Everett. Illustrator and author of picture books, novels, and perhaps best known for his illustrated informational books. Fisher uses a variety of art styles. For two biographies he used acrylic paintings to create black and white illustrations: *Madame Curie* (Macmillan, 1994) and *Ghandi* (Atheneum, 1995).

Gibbons, Gail. Illustrator and author whose vibrant illustrations and clear text make concepts accessible to young children. *The Planets* (Holiday House, 1993) was ranked an outstanding first reader. Her other titles from Holiday House include *Deserts* (1996), *The Honey Makers* (1997), and *Soaring with the Wind: The Bald Eagle* (1998).

Giblin, James Cross. An author who takes ordinary subjects and turns them into fascinating histories that cut across cultures. Source notes, bibliographies, and extensive indexes add to the informative nature of his titles and reflect his research efforts. Sample titles are *Be Seated: A Book About Chairs* (HarperCollins 1993) and *When Plague Strikes: The Black Death, Smallpox, AIDS* (HarperCollins 1995).

Hoban, Tana. Photographer and author who creates photographic images that introduce concepts to young children. Her books invite the child to participate as in *Look Book* (Greenwillow, 1997), which includes holes for the child to look through and anticipate what the next picture will be.

Lewin, Ted. Illustrator and author whose fictional and informational works reflect his interests in conservation and global travel. His illustrations give a sense of time and place as in *Ali: Child of the Desert* by Jonathan London (Lothrop, 1997); *Fair!* (Lothrop, 1997) and *The Always Prayer Shawl* by Sheldon Oberman (Boyds Mills, 1994).

Meltzer, Milton. Historian and biographer who writes within the context of social concerns and clearly distinguishes fact from fiction as in *Hold Your Horses! A Feedbag Full of Fact and Fable* (HarperCollins, 1995). His characteristic use of primary documents (excerpts from letters, diaries, newspapers, speeches, and other original documents) is evident in *Frederick Douglass: In His Own Words* (Harcourt, 1995).

Miller, Margaret. Photographer and author of *Now I'm Big* (Greenwillow 1996) and *Big and Little* (Greenwillow, 1998) and photographer for titles by Joanna Cole. See Cole, Joanna.

Morris, Ann. Author of a photoessay series about common activities around the world. The index identifies the location of the photograph's setting and briefly explains the activity. The final page in each book is a global map showing the location of the settings of the photographs. *Play* and *Work* (Lothrop, Lee & Shepard, 1998) is a representative title.

Parker, Nancy Winslow. Illustrator and author who uses bold, stylized, two-dimensional pictures to bring information books to younger readers. Representative works include *Money, Money, Money: The Meaning of the Art and Symbols on United States Paper Currency* (HarperCollins 1995) and *Locks, Crocs, & Skeeters: The Story of the Panama Canal* (Greenwillow, 1996).

Chapter 11

Applying Criteria to Particular Subjects

> *Only when a book is written out of . . .*
> *passion is there much hope of its being*
> *read with passion. Children, above all,*
> *need to feel that they are partners in the*
> *quest.*
>
> —Jean Fritz,
> "Partners in the Quest for Truth."

In addition to criteria identified in earlier chapters, there are unique characteristics pertaining to books on particular subjects that call for additional consideration when selecting these books. Subjects covered in this chapter include biography, visual arts, how-to-do-it books, science and technology, social sciences, and mathematics.

SPECIAL CRITERIA FOR SUBJECT AREAS

Biography

Biography is a history of a person's life written by someone else who has researched and read about the person in order to portray the individual's life accurately and interestingly. A person writes an **autobiography** about his or her own life. A well-written biography is a social history, and like historical fiction it should reflect the values and attitudes consistent with the time period covered.

Common elements in a biography are facts, an overriding concept or theme, and the writer's interest in and enthusiasm for the subject. Characteristics of a well-written biography are realistic, believable dialogue and accurate information. Jean Fritz's biographies about Paul Revere and Sam Adams exemplify these qualities. Teachers use biographies to teach about other times, provide role models, and demonstrate examples of setting personal goals.

As you think about biographies, consider a cautionary note from Betsy Harvey Kraft, author of *Mother Jones: One Woman's Fight for Labor*, who reminds us that "with any historic figure, it is often hard to separate fact from fiction" (Kraft, 1995:3).

Biographies for children, like those for adults, include a variety of types ranging from authentic to fictionalized biography. The writer of **authentic biographies** follows the same rules as those used in scholarly works for adults. The author provides documentation for sources of information such as letters, diaries, videotape recordings, and eyewitness accounts. Conversations are limited to known statements by the individuals. Russell Freedman's works fall into this category.

Authors of **fictionalized biographies** also base their telling on careful research. In this type of biography, the author personalizes the subject and creates dramatic episodes through the use of imagined conversations or through expression of the character's thoughts.

Biographies vary in coverage of their subject. The most comprehensive ones, called **complete biographies**, cover the subject's life from birth to death, such as Russell Freedman's *Lincoln: A Photobiography*. **Partial biographies** focus on one period, one event, or a characteristic of the subject. An example is *Stranded at Plimouth Plantation, 1626*, which uses a journal format to depict the life of a thirteen-year-old.

In **picture-book biographies** illustrations play a dominant role in presenting the information. Diane Stanley's illustrations capture the historical period, the society in which the subject lived, and the artwork of the period.

Children also enjoy reading autobiographies, such as Sid Fleishman's *The Abracadabra Kid: A Writer's Life*. Collective biographies usually present brief sketches of several individuals. The biographies may share a common theme, be about people in similar situations, or be about individuals unrelated to each other.

CRITERIA

Selection of biographical works involves applying the criteria for fiction (see Chapter 6), picture book as format (see Chapter 5), and information works (see Chapter 10). In addition, consider the following questions:

- For the biography of an individual, can the reader access a particular period of importance in the subject's life?
- Is the subject's life distorted by significant omissions?
- Is the setting authentic?

- Does the person have believable values?
- Does the person face a believable problem or goal?
- Is there a sequence of factual events that leads to an achievement or contribution? Or, on the other hand to trials and tribulations?
- Does the narrative have a theme or universal truth?
- Does the writer express or imply why the subject was chosen?
- Does the author use a suitable tone and an appropriate style?
- How is the material organized in a collective biography? Is it easy to identify the section about a particular person?
- If the collective biography has a theme, how effectively is the author able to maintain that theme?
- For a collective biography, does the author indicate the criteria used to select the entries? Do the subjects meet the criteria?
- Does the use of quotations or dialogue bring the subject to life without disrupting the flow of the text?
- Does the author create a believable person, one with strengths and weaknesses?
- Does the author avoid manipulating facts to make a more interesting story? Does the author avoid didactic writing and stressing particular values and attitudes?
- Does the author avoid overly glamorizing the individual?
- Does the subject's life offer interest and meaning for today's child?
- In a fictionalized biography, does the author inform the reader about which statements, dates, places, and names are true and which are not?
- In fictionalized biographies is the narrator's point of view appropriate and does it add to the story?

With the growth of visual literacy and the increasing number of picture book biographies Joanna Rudge Long points out other considerations:

> How accessible are style and visual references for the intended audience? Are pictorial motifs used in appropriate contexts? Are they sourced? Like words, pictures convey attitudes and points of view—are these in harmony with the subject's true spirit? (Long, 1997:48)

The Visual Arts

Current art books focus on one of the following: (1) basic art elements or books about visual perception, (2) art history, or (3) a single topic, such as the biography of an artist, information about a specific genre, or works from an art movement. Again, each focus needs to be evaluated in terms of how effectively it fulfills its purpose for the intended audience.

CRITERIA

- What is the quality of the reproductions?
- Is the format of the book manageable?
- Is the book organized chronologically, thematically, or by subject?
- Are women artists and members of other cultures included?
- How skillful is the author in involving the reader in looking, learning, and appreciating?
- Does the text offer more than brief facts?
- Does the book provide information about the present location of art originals?

How-To-Do-It Books (Crafts, Art, Sewing, Cooking, Sports)

Activity books or those designed to inform children about how to make or do something call for special criteria. According to Dixie Lee Spiegel, a test for activity books is that

> children should be able to complete the activities with a minimum of adult supervision or assistance. The materials and set-up for activities may require some adult preparation (Spiegel, 1991: 594).

Books dealing with magic, chemistry, and cooking should warn about hazards. According to Pat Manning and Alan R. Newman

> Kids not only often do not *know* about safety risks, they don't even *think* [italics in original] about the hazards they do know. Young readers have also been known to bleep over directions and warnings to get to the fun parts of an experiment (Manning and Newman, 1986: 101).

They recommend Vicky Cobb's science experiment books, which rely on common household ingredients.

CRITERIA

Other criteria to consider:

- Are the directions complete and clearly written?
- Will the child be able to transfer the skills or strategies learned in the activity to another situation?
- Are there sufficient examples for the child to learn the skill or strategy?
- Is the activity worthwhile?
- Does the intended audience have the appropriate skills to perform the activities suggested?

- Is there a list of all materials and equipment that will be needed?
- Are these materials accessible to children using this book?
- Do instructions include safety rules and precautions?
- Do illustrations show each step in the process?
- Do illustrations show children doing age-appropriate procedures and adults performing more dangerous procedures?
- Do the projects encourage creativity?
- Is the finished product worth making?
- Does a cookbook provide nutritional information?
- Does the cookbook offer information about healthy eating plans?
- Are statistics used judiciously without bombarding the reader?

Science and Technology

Teachers who use children's literature in teaching science find these books have many advantages. The books focus on content, and the students develop an appreciation for science-based literature. These books also help children improve reading skills while they are learning about scientific principles. The literature then enhances the child's general understanding of the world. In addition, the books can provide for individual differences as different books match a given child's learning patterns and areas of interest.

Keeping up on developments in the fields of science and technology is a constant challenge. However, without knowledge of the field it is hard to know if the information in the books one is selecting is accurate. Fortunately, there are a number of helpful sources. Sara Inbody Flowers recommends using *Odyssey*, a magazine for children, as a way to keep up with space science (Flowers, 1992: 38). In the reviewing journal *Appraisal: Science Books for Young People* you can compare the reviews by a subject specialist and a librarian. The American Association for the Advancement of Science's *Science Books and Films* also offers reviews by subject specialists.

Not only are developments within the field changing, but social concerns also add to the need for accurate, up-to-date, information in science books. In addressing the impact of the application of technology to the reproductive process and the real dangers of AIDS, Melissa Gross argues

> Children need information about homosexuality, sexual abuse, sexually transmitted disease, and contraception. . . . The need for timely information can not be overstressed. Even very current books about AIDS have been found to give the mistaken impression that it is primarily a homosexual problem. Such misinformation can be deadly (Gross, 1995: 214).

Gross also stresses the need for books to be objective and action oriented, to make the reader aware of peer pressure, and to explain how to say "no".

In the area of natural sciences there are some concepts that should be avoided:

- **Oversimplification**, concepts should not be confused with facts.
- **Anthropomorphism**, presenting animals as though they have human characteristics. Such personification may be appropriate for poetry and fiction but not for science.
- **Teleology**, ascribing purpose to something in the natural environment.
- **Animism**, attributing conscious life and spirit to natural forms such as plants and rocks.

CRITERIA

- Is the information accurate?
- Is the depth and coverage of the information appropriate for the intended audience?
- Is terminology accurate, avoiding slang or euphemism?
- Does the author present the social and political issues involved?
- Does the author explain that science is a process, one to which the reader may contribute in the future?
- Do books about experiments use the discovery method? Do they stress observation of scientific method, keeping records, and drawing inferences from conclusions?
- Is symbolic language interpreted?
- Are scientific abbreviations explained?
- Are graphs and diagrams explained?
- Are directions complete and clearly written?
- Is safety stressed?
- Are safety risks identified?
- Does the author warn about poisons or human toxicities and suggest antidotes?
- Are the ingredients recommended for use in experiments commonly found at home?
- Are opinion and fact clearly differentiated?
- Are generalizations tested?
- Does the author explain the relationship between steps in an experiment?
- Is the book designed to teach or only to entertain?
- Do the visuals provide information about scientific laws and principles, or are they merely attractive?
- Are correct anatomical terms used?
- Are topics such as the physical and psychological aspects of puberty treated in an objective and unemotional way?
- Does the author present different attitudes about topics such as contraception?
- Does the collection include books offering different viewpoints and values?

Social Sciences

In the social studies curriculum, teachers use children's literature books to build vocabulary, provide new experiences, make connections among subjects within the curriculum, provide problem-solving situations, have children engage in research, and help them develop appreciation for informational literature. As one example, Linda K. Rogers and Karen Bromley write about the value of using children's books to develop geographic literacy. They suggest that

> teachers identify the settings of stories (e.g., location, place, and/or regions), show students where the story takes place in relation to their own location, and explain the unique characteristics of a place and/or region (Rogers and Bromley, 1995:1).

According to the *Curriculum Standards for Social Studies: Expectations of Excellence*, the primary purpose of social studies education is

> to help young people develop the ability to make informed and reasoned decisions for the public good as citizens of a culturally diverse, democratic society in an interdependent world (National Council for the Social Studies, 1994: vii).

The content involves the social sciences and the humanities. It draws on the

> *disciplines of anthropology, archaeology, economics, geography, history, law, philosophy, political science, psychology, religion and sociology, as well as appropriate content from the humanities, mathematics, and natural sciences* [original in italics] (National Council for the Social Studies, *1994: 3*).

The standards are organized around ten thematic strands drawing from one or more disciplines.

Theme 1. Culture: recognize and accept the concepts of likeness and differences.

Theme 2. Time, Continuity, and Change: see relationships.

Theme 3. People, Places, and Environments: observe how environment influences different people in different places.

Theme 4. Individual Development and Identity: understand development of personal identity and the influences that shape it.

Theme 5. Individuals, Groups, and Institutions; know how institutions are formed and changed; how they influence individuals; what institutions are; and the potential for conflicts among them.

Theme 6. Power, Authority, and Governance: understand how people create and change structures of power, authority, and governance.

Theme 7. Production, Distribution, and Consumption: learn how societies organize to meet wants and needs with limited resources.

Theme 8. Science, Technology, and Society: understand relationships among these subjects.

Theme 9. Global Connections: study the interdependence of people and places on earth including the far-reaching consequences of actions or interactions by individuals or groups upon the environment. The natural and physical sciences provide important contributing data to this theme.

Theme 10. Civic Ideals and Practices: explore citizenship in a democratic society; study the ideals, principles, and practices including views of citizenship in other times and places.

The "Notable Children's Trade Books in the Field of Social Studies" for 1997 identifies the appropriateness of each of its recommended titles to the thematic strands of the Social Studies Standards. (Children's Book Council and National Council for the Social Studies, 1997: unp) Examples of titles on the list are Mary Lankford's *Jacks around the World* to illustrate concepts of global likenesses and Allen Say's *Grandfather's Journey* to show relationships of past and present.

Mathematics

The mathematics curriculum also has undergone changes with opportunities to use children's literature more extensively than in earlier curricular movements. In *Read Any Good Math Lately?* David J. Whitin and Sandra Wilde describe fiction and information books to use. The goals for students in the *Curriculum and Evaluation Standards for School Mathematics* include

- valuing mathematics as a "common human activity" (Whitin and Wilde, 1992:4),
- communicating with the language of mathematics,
- engaging in activities "related to the cultural, historical and scientific evolution of mathematics" (Whitin and Wilde, 1992:6),
- developing number sense, and
- engaging in problem posing.

These are aspects recommended in the standards.

As you select mathematics books consider how effective they will be in helping the reader with the skills listed above. Also remember that mathematical concepts can be found in folklore, fiction, and yes, even poetry. For the latter see *Marvelous Math: A Book of Poems* selected by Lee Bennett Hopkins.

An example of a series developed to correlate with the curriculum standards is the MathStart series published by HarperCollins. Each book includes math-related activities using readily available materials. The series focuses on how math is used in our everyday lives.

Traditionally many of our mathematics collections have been limited to counting books, and these still are an important part of our collection for younger children. Representative titles are identified at the end of the chapter.

CRITERIA

- Do visual and verbal statements tell the reader what is to be counted or manipulated?
- Are the directions clear and organized in logical steps?
- Do the text and illustrations match?
- In counting books is there an open space around the numerals and objects?
- How are sets or groupings differentiated?
- Do the counting books show objects with which a child is familiar?
- In a narrative how does the author avoid losing the number concept or manipulation in the text?
- Do the illustrations give meaning to abstract mathematical principles?
- Does the book relate its content to everyday life?
- Does the content encourage interactive readers?
- How well does the book fulfill the criteria listed earlier in this chapter for how-to-do-it books?
- Do the endpapers and the cover provide clues to the content or reveal content?
- Does the collection include books about mathematical games and puzzles?

SUMMARY

The unique characteristics of individual subjects call for additional considerations in their selection. Changes in nationally adopted curriculum guidelines and standards influence the characteristics one seeks in books on a particular subject. Other criteria are generated for the need to present safety features or warnings. Accuracy is a basic criterion for all these books.

TITLES MENTIONED IN THIS CHAPTER

The Abracadabra Kid: A Writer's Life by Sid Fleishman. Greenwillow, 1996.
And Then What Happened Paul Revere? by Jean Fritz. Putnam, 1973.
Appraisal: Science Books for Young People. Boston University School of Education, Children's Science Book Review Committee, Department of Science and Mathematics, 1967–

Grandfather's Journey by Allen Say. Houghton Mifflin, 1993.

Jacks around the World by Mary Lankford. Morrow, 1996.

Lincoln: A Photobiography by Russell Freedman. Clarion, 1987.

Marvelous Math: A Book of Poems selected by Lee Bennett Hopkins, illustrated by Karen Barbour. Simon & Schuster, 1997.

MathStart series, edited by Stuart J. Murphy. Level 1, for ages three years and up, is about counting, ordering, recognizing patterns, and comparing sizes. Level 2, for first grade and up, is about basic mathematics skills, such as adding subtracting, reading timelines, and estimating. Level 3, for second grade and up, is about multiplying, dividing, building equations, and problem-solving strategies. New York: HarperCollins.

Mother Jones: One Woman's Fight for Labor by Betsy Harvey Kraft. Clarion, 1995.

Odyssey. Cobblestone, 1992–

Science Books and Films. American Association for the Advancement of Science, 1975–

Stranded at Plimouth, 1626 by Gary Bowen. HarperCollins, 1994.

Why Don't You Get a Horse, Sam Adams? by Jean Fritz. Putnam, 1977.

REFERENCES

Boulanger, Susan. 1996. "Language, Imagination, Vision: Art Books for Children," *Horn Book Magazine* 72, no. 3 (May-June): 295–304.

Bromley, Karen D'Angelo. 1996. *Webbing with Literature: Creating Story Maps with Children's Books.* 2nd ed. Boston: Allyn and Bacon.

Cornog, Martha, and Timothy Perper. 1996. *For Sex Education, See Librarian: A Guide to Issues and Resources.* Westport, Conn.: Greenwood Press.

Fallon, Michael. 1993. "Science Teaching '90s Style." *Instructor* 102 (March): 24–25.

Flowers, Sarah Inbody. 1992. "The Big Bang: The Information Explosion on the Solar System." *School Library Journal* 38, no. 11 (November): 37–38.

Fritz, Jean. Nd. "Partners in the Quest for Truth," *The Basics of Writing for Children and Young Adults* 11: 70.

Gath, Tracy. 1995. "Science Books & Films Celebrate 30 Years" *Science Books & Films* 31, no. 3 (April): 65–67, 90.

Gross, Melissa. 1995. "Sex Education Books for Kids, Grades K-6." *Journal of Youth Services in Libraries* 8, no. 2 (Winter): 213–216.

Kirkpatrick, Carole. 1993. "Who's in the Kitchen? Cookbooks for Kids." *School Library Journal* 39, no. 4 (April): 42–43.

Krey, De An M. 1995. "Operationalizing the Thematic Strands of Social Studies for Young Learners." *Social Studies and the Young Learner* 8, no. 1 (September/October): 12–15.

Long, Joanna Rudge. 1997. "Eloquent Visions: Perspectives in Picture Book Biography." *School Library Journal* (April): 48–49.

Madrazo, Gerry M. Jr. 1997. "Using Trade Books to Teach and Learn Science." *Science and Children* 34, no.6 (March): 20–21.

Manning, Pat, and Alan R. Newman. 1986. "Safety Isn't Always First: A Disturbing Look at Chemistry Books." *School Library Journal* 33, no. 2 (October): 99–102.

———. 1992. "The World of 1492 in Company with Columbus." *School Library Journal* 38, no. 2 (February): 26–30.

McMath, Joan, and Margaret King. 1993. "Open Books, Open Minds." *Science and Children* 30 (February): 33–37.

Meltzer, Milton. 1986. "Notes on Biography." *Children's Literature Quarterly.* 10, no. 4 (Winter): 172–175.

Murphy, Stuart J. 1996. "MathStart in the Making." *Book Links* 5, no. 6 (July): 25–29.

National Council for the Social Studies. 1994. *Curriculum Standards for Social Studies: Expectations of Excellence.* The Council.

National Council of Teachers of Mathematics. 1989. *Curriculum and Evaluation Standards for School Mathematics.* The Council.

Nicols, Danita. 1993. "Math Concept Books: What We Have, What We Need." *School Library Journal* 39, no. 12 (December): 41–42.

Rayno, Chet. 1992. "Dr. Seuss and Dr. Einstein: Children's Books and Scientific Imagination." *Horn Book Magazine* (Sept./Oct.): 560–567.

Rogers, Linda K., and Karen Bromley. 1995. "Developing Geographic Literacy: An Annotated List of Children's Literature." *Social Studies and the Young Learners* 8, no. 2 (November/December): 1–3.

Saul, Wendy, and Sybille A. Jagusch, eds. 1991. *Vital Connections: Children, Science, and Books.* Papers from a Symposium sponsored by the Children's Literature Center. Washington, D.C.: Library of Congress.

Spiegel, Dixie Lee. 1991. "Children's Activity Books." *Reading Teacher* 44, no. 8 (April): 594–596.

Stull, Elizabeth C. 1998. "Taking a New Look at Alphabet Books in the '90s." *Book Links* 7, no. 4(March): 26–30.

Whitin, David J. 1992. "Explore Mathematics through Children's Literature." *School Library Journal* 38, no. 8 (August): 24–28.

Whitin, David J., and Sandra Wilde. 1992. *Read Any Good Math Lately? Children's Books for Mathematical Learning, K-6.* Portsmouth, N.H.: Heinemann.

Wilton, Shirley. 1993. "Reviewing Art Books: Reflections and Projections." *School Library Journal* 39, no. 1 (January): 34–35.

Wunder, Susan. 1995. "Addressing the Standards for Social Studies with Children's Literature." *Social Studies and the Young Learner* 8, no. 2 (November/December): 4–7.

RECOMMENDED PROFESSIONAL RESOURCES

Bounce, Barbara, and Wendy Saul. 1994. *Exploring Space: Using Seymour Simon's Astronomy Books in the Classroom.* New York: Morrow.

Describes individual and group activities for children using Simon's books and books by other authors. Includes colored photographs from NASA and the National Optical Astronomy Observatories.

Cornog, Martha, and Timothy Perper. 1996. *For Sex Education, See Librarian: A Guide to Issues and Resources.* Westport, Conn.: Greenwood.

Discusses selecting, processing, and making materials accessible. Provides annotated bibliographic entries for over 600 recommended books for school and public libraries.

Kobrin, Beverly. 1995. *Eyeopeners II: Children's Books to Answer Children's Questions about the World around Them.* Scholastic.

Provides descriptive annotations for over 800 titles and suggested activities for some of them. The book is arranged by subject and the "Quick-Link Index" (a subject index). Identifies related titles listed under other subjects. Includes an index of authors, illustrators, and book titles.

Science Books & Films. ISSN 0098–342X. Nine times per year (monthly, except January/February, June/July, and August/September are combined) by the American Association for the Advancement of Science, 1333 H St. NW, Washington, DC 20005.

Covers books, films, videos, software, and CD-ROMs for all ages including science professionals. Uses a starring system for recommended books and rates others as acceptable or not recommended.

Simonson, Sara, Stacy Curry, and Molly White. 1996. "Angles on Geometry." *Book Links* 6, no. 2 (November): 25–30.

Offers suggested activities for teachers to use with recommended titles about exploring geometry,

Whitin, David J., and Sandra Wilde. 1996. *It's the Story That Counts: More Children's Books for Mathematical Learning, K-6.* Portsmouth, N.H.: Heinemann.

———. 1992. *Read Any Good Math Lately? Children's Books for Mathematical Learning, K-6.* Portsmouth, N.H.: Heineman.

Zarnowski, Myra, and Arlene F. Gallagher, eds. 1993. *Children's Literature and Social Studies: Selecting and Using Notable Books in the Classroom.* Dubuque, Iowa:Kendall/Hunt. Provides criteria for selecting children's books and describes how to use them in social studies units.

REPRESENTATIVE COUNTING BOOKS

Anno's Counting Book by Anno Mitsumasa (Crowell 1977).
  One of the few counting books to include zero. Includes concept of sets and change of seasons. The watercolor pictures enhance this wordless book. For a more complex work see *Anno's Magic Seeds* (Philomel, 1995).
The Lifesize Animal Counting Book (Dorling Kindersley, 1994).
  Life-size photographs of animals add to the appeal of this book.
Moja Means One: Swahili Counting Book by Muriel L. Feelings, illustrated by Tom Feelings (Dial 1971).
  A resourceful visual and textual introduction to East African rural life and to the phonetic pronunciation of Swahili words.
More Than One by Miriam Schlein, illustrated by Donald Crews (Greenwillow, 1996).
  Explores the concept of number one, which can refer to one item or more as found in one baseball team of nine players.
Roman Numerals I to MM by Arthur Geisert (Houghton Mifflin, 1996).
  Counting Geisert's well-known pigs leads to finding the number that is the value of the roman numeral.
Uno, Dos, Tres: One, Two, Three by Pat Mora, illustrated by Barbara Lavallee (Clarion, 1996).
  An English and Spanish text tells the story of two sisters going to market to look for gifts for their mother.
Who's Counting by Nancy Tafuri (Greenwillow, 1986).
  Bold, stylized double-page spreads depict animals, including a golden retriever puppy, for the young observer to find.

REPRESENTATIVE TITLES OF OTHER INFORMATION BOOKS

The Big Bug Book by Margery Facklam illustrated with life size drawings by Paul Facklam (Little, 1994). Shows the size of the bug in relation to common objects in a home.
De Colores and Other Latin-American Folk Songs for Children selected, arranged, and translated by Jose-Luis Orozco, illustrated by Elisa Kleven (Dutton, 1994). Bilingual text with music for songs from Panama, Paraguay, Mexico, Ecuador, and Nicaragua.
The Good Housekeeping Illustrated Children's Cookbook by Marianne Zanarella with photographs by Tom Eckerle (Morrow, 1997).
  Discusses importance of cleaning up and safety practices. Provides time (preparation, cooking, and total); difficulty of recipe; the number of servings; utensils; ingredients; and steps involved. An illustrated glossary, photographs of the utensils, and an index make the information accessible.
It's Perfectly Normal: Changing Bodies, Growing Up, Sex & Sexual Health by Robie H. Harris, illustrated by Michael Emberley (Candlewick, 1994). With a

sense of humor this book objectively addresses a wide range of topics including homosexuality, sexual abuse, and sexually transmitted diseases.

Lives of the Writers: Comedies, Tragedies (and What the Neighbors Thought) by Kathleen Krull and illustrated by Kathryn Hewitt (Harcourt Brace, 1994) and *Lives of the Musicians: Good Times, Bad Times* offer brief but witty portrayals of the subjects.

Mother Jones: One Woman's Fight for Labor by Betsy Harvey Kraft (Clarion, 1995). A well-paced telling of the history of the labor movement and of Mary Harris Jones' life, is enriched with photographs and reproductions of illustrations from the era.

The World in 1492 (Holt, 1992) by Jean Fritz, Katherine Paterson, Patricia and Fredrick McKissack, Margaret Mahy, and Jamake Highwater is a world history that portrays what was going on in the world besides Christopher Columbus' voyage.

REPRESENTATIVE AUTHORS AND ILLUSTRATORS

Arnold, Caroline. Author of fiction and information books, who frequently does natural science titles with Richard Hewett as photographer. Their series More Animal Favorites (Morrow) for third to sixth graders has a 48-page text with an index for animals including *Sea Lion* (1994), *Rhino* (1995), and *Bats* (1996).

Cobb, Vicki. Author who encourages children to experiment with science in their everyday lives. Examples of titles are *Science Experiments You Can Eat*, revised and updated (HarperCollins, 1994), *Don't Try This at Home! Science Fun for Kids on the Go* with Kathy Darling (Morrow, 1998).

Cooper, Floyd. Author and illustrator of books with African American backgrounds. Two biographies he wrote are *Mandela, From the Life of the South African Statesman* (Philomel, 1996) and *Coming Home, From the Life of Langston Hughes* (Philomel, 1994). Cooper was illustrator for Nancy Lamb and the Children of Oklahoma City's *One April Morning: Children Remember the Oklahoma City Bombing* (Lothrop, Lee & Shepard, 1996), a book for which his realistic, softly toned oil illustrations make a fitting complement. The folksong *Cumbayah* (Morrow, 1998) includes the music.

Freedman, Russell. Nonfiction writer of science, American history, and biography. As in his other biographies, in *Eleanor Roosevelt: A Life of Discovery* (Clarion, 1993) he identifies his sources of information and photographs, uses direct quotations, provides bibliographies, identifies places to visit to learn more about the subject, and includes an index of people, places, and subjects.

Fritz, Jean. Author known for historical fiction and biographies, enlivening history, and making it accessible to young children. *Surprising Myself* (Richard C. Owen, 1992) is rated as an outstanding first reader. A representative title for older readers is *You Want Women to Vote, Lizzie Stanton?* (Putnam, 1995).

Lavies, Bianca. A photographer with an astute eye who chronicles the behavior and life cycles of animals and brings her reader close to the subjects as in *A*

Gathering of Garter Snakes (Dutton, 1993). She concludes books with a page describing her experiences as a photographer of the subject.

Lankford, Mary D. Author who brings other cultures to readers through her books about games and events shared throughout the world. The books typically include a world map, directions for playing the game in each of the represented countries, a bibliography, and an index. Examples are *Jacks around the World* (Morrow, 1996) and *Dominoes around the World* (Morrow, 1998), both illustrated by Karen Dugan.

Lipsyte, Robert. Prize-winning sports columnist and author of biographies for third through sixth graders. Titles include *Joe Louis: A Champ for All America* (HarperCollins, 1993) and *Michael Jordan: A Life above the Rim* (HarperCollins, 1994).

Markle, Sandra. Author of the Outside and Inside series on animals (e.g., *Outside and Inside Alligators*, Atheneum, 1998) and activity books on science and mathematics (e.g., *Measuring Up: Experiments, Puzzles, and Games Exploring Measurement*, Atheneum, 1995). They are clearly written with informative, captioned, and colorful illustrations. The experiments move from simple to challenging. The glossaries, pronunciation guides, and indexes make these accessible to children.

McMillan, Bruce. Photographer and author known for his technically fine and almost poetic pictures of nature. In *Summer Ice: Life along the Antarctic Peninsula* (Houghton, 1995) the placement of close-ups within a broader context give additional meaning to the text. Maps, a glossary, a bibliography, his notes about the photographs, plus an index make this an informative resource.

Micklethwait, Lucy. Author whose I Spy series and Spot a . . . series link art with various topics. The books are designed to have children look for familiar objects in a wide range of paintings from different cultures.

Murphy, Jim. Author who portrays the feelings of the people involved in an event. At the same time he effectively uses and cites sources of illustrations (maps, photographs, other documents). These illustrations are from the historical period and help document and tell the story. A map repeated throughout the book provides a timeline in *The Great Fire* (Scholastic, 1995).

Patent, Dorothy Hinshaw. Author about animals. Her books have bibliographies with titles for young readers, indexes, and glossaries. She used William Munoz's photography in *Deer and Elk* (Clarion 1994), *Prairies* (Holiday House, 1996), and *Fire: Friend or Foe* (Clarion, 1998).

Pringle, Lawrence. Author and editor on biological and environmental subjects and about people who work in those fields. He writes in an objective manner, provides glossaries, and identifies agencies and organizations that the reader may want to consult. Representative titles include *Vanishing Ozone: Protecting Earth from Ultraviolet Radiation* (A Save the Earth series, Morrow, 1995); *Elephant Woman: Cynthia Moss Explores the World of Elephants* (Atheneum, 1997); *Smoking: A Risky Business* (Morrow, 1996); and *Drinking: A Risky Business* (Morrow, 1997).

Simon, Seymour. Science writer who acknowledges what we know and distinguishes it from what is theory while indicating how information changes. Typically his books are oversize with full-color illustrations and a clear text. Representative titles include *The Brain: Our Nervous System* (Morrow, 1997), *Muscles: Our Muscular System* (Morrow, 1998), and *Bones: Our Skeletal System* (Morrow, 1998).

Stanley, Diane. Illustrator and author with a sense of design. Stanley creates detailed illustrations, borders, and costumes from the period of the biography or setting of the folktale. With her husband Peter Vennema she wrote *Cleopatra* (Morrow, 1994) and *Leonardo da Vinci* (Morrow, 1996).

Zeldis, Malcah. Illustrator whose folk art appears in *Martin Lurther King* by Rosemary L. Bray (Greenwillow, 1995) and *Eve and Her Sisters: Women of the Old Testament* by Yona Zeldis McDonough (Greenwillow, 1994).

Chapter 12

Selecting Reference Books

A child's search for information may be linked to completing a school assignment, answering a personal problem, or satisfying an intellectual curiosity. Whatever the purpose, children have the same right to quality reference service as adults.
—Vicky L. Crosson,
"Hey! Kids Are Patrons, Too!"

In an elementary school any title in the collection may be used to answer a specific question or provide information about a subject. The focus in this chapter is on titles designed to supply answers to reference questions. These books may present a broad overview of a subject or specific facts. Easy access to the information is a highly desirable feature. Reference books are not designed for consecutive reading, although children have been known to try to read a multivolume encyclopedia from A to Z.

Students consult reference books for answers to different types of questions:

1. **ready reference questions**, the student wants specific information such as a fact,
2. **search questions**, the student is developing a short report and wants to consult several sources (a chapter in a book, an encyclopedia article, or short magazine article), or
3. **research questions**, the student will investigate the subject more thoroughly and use many sources.

These titles are often shelved in a specific area and labeled "Noncirculating—Reference Use Only." Duplicate copies of some titles may be necessary to provide for daily reference questions and for circulation. For example, a field guide to rocks may be needed as a source for a field trip and simultaneously in the media center.

GENERAL CRITERIA FOR ALL REFERENCE BOOKS

As you evaluate reference books, consider these questions:

Authority

- What are the credentials of the editors, who are responsible for policies on what information will be included as well as for the format of the book?
- Are the qualifications of the authors, consultants, and contributors listed in the introduction or preface?
- Are their qualifications appropriate for the subjects covered in this reference work?
- Has the author or editor worked on similar projects? If so, how successful were those projects?
- Are the sources of information acknowledged?
- Are those reliable sources?

Scope

- Is the purpose of the work stated in the title, the introduction, or the preface?
- Does that purpose meet instructional or personal needs?
- Does the work fulfill its stated purpose?
- In examining the index can you judge the range and depth of coverage?
- What subject matter is the focus of this work?
- Does the work provide an overview or an in-depth coverage of the topic?
- What are the stated limitations?
- How does this book differ from similar works?

Accuracy

- When you check facts such as population figures, geographical boundaries, or names currently in the news is the information in the book up-to-date?
- When you compare dates, facts, illustrative materials, and statistics with other sources do you find the information to be accurate and up-to-date?

- Does the information appear to be thorough, reliable, and complete?
- Are items in the bibliographies recent?

Treatment of Material

- Are facts distinguished from opinions?
- Are controversial issues presented?
- Are both sides of controversial issues presented?
- Is the content presented in a logical and objective manner?
- Are subjects of equal importance given equal space?
- Are instructions for how to use the book clearly written?
- Have foreign names been translated into English?

Arrangement

- Is the book arranged by alphabetical, chronological, classified, geographical, tabular, topical, or statistical order?
- Is the arrangement clear and appropriate for the purpose of the reference work?
- Is it easy to access the information?

Reputation of Author, Editor, Illustrator, and Publisher

- What is the reputation and expertise of individuals responsible for this book?
- Are works by this publisher listed in selected bibliographies or standard reviewing media?
- Does the publisher have a commitment to this type of reference work?

Special Features

- Do charts, tables, and maps have explanatory captions?
- Are the subject headings appropriate for both the child and the adult user?
- Are cross-references provided?
- Is there a pronunciation guide?
- Is there a glossary of the terms used in the reference work?
- Does the book contain appendices?
- Are there author, illustrator, title, series, subject, and other appropriate indexes?
- Does the index list all place names that appear on the maps?
- Are the indexes adequate?
- Does the index identify the exact map, latitude, longitude, and grid information needed to locate a specific place on a map?
- Are there other special features that would help young users?

Audience

- Is the reading level and comprehension level appropriate for children?
- Is the subject of interest to children?

Format

- Is the binding strong enough for the size and weight of the volume and for use by children?
- Can children handle the weight, shape, and size of the book?
- Can you open a volume so the pages are flat and a two-page spread is not lost in the binding?
- Is a variety of type sizes and spacing used to set off different sections?
- Is the typeface clear and readable?
- Are the contents clearly indicated on the outside of the volume?
- Does the format facilitate use of the book?
- Are the illustrations numerous, accurate, and recent?
- Are graphs clearly labeled?
- Is the paper opaque enough so that the type does not show through?
- Are distinctive headings and subheadings within a page used to isolate or highlight information, making it easier to find?
- Is a large type version available for use by those with visual problems?
- Is lettering readable?

Aesthetic Qualities

- Are illustrations informative and appealing?
- Are colors used to provide information and appeal?
- Do the illustrations relate to the text?
- Are the illustrations clear, current, and identified?
- Are the illustrations placed appropriately in relation to the text?
- Does the set have an attractive design and layout?
- Will the graphic design appeal to and be appropriate for the intended audience?

Multicultural Aspects

- Are the illustrations ethnically sensitive?
- Does the information reflect ethnic cultures and lifestyles?
- Are racist concepts, cliches, phrases, or words avoided?
- Are major events of ethnic history covered?
- Does the information acknowledge the diversity of subgroups within minority groups?
- Is the reference work free of denigrating language?

- Is the overuse of the pronoun "he" avoided?
- Is single gender characterization for vocations avoided?

Comparison

- Does the reference work offer features not found in similar books?
- Is the price appropriate for the book's anticipated use and quality?

SPECIAL CRITERIA FOR PARTICULAR TYPES OF REFERENCE

Almanacs and Yearbooks

An **almanac** is an annual or biennial compendium of data and statistics relating to countries, personalities, events, and subjects. The information is brief and may cover recent or retrospective events of the past decade or longer.

Since much of the information in almanacs comes from government documents or other primary sources, the almanac can serve as an index to those sources. Almanacs also serve as directories with their lists of names and addresses for associations and societies.

The **yearbook** or **annual** is also a compendium of data and statistics. The information is limited to occurrences of the previous year; no attempt is made to cover retrospective information as in the almanac. A yearbook is often used to supplement and update an encyclopedia. Another type of annual publication deals with events, holidays, and anniversaries.

A **compendium** is a brief summary of a larger work or of a field of knowledge. One example is the *Statistical Abstract of the United States,* a summary of data in the U.S. Bureau of the Census reports.

Geographical Sources

A map is a representation of the earth, moon, or another planet usually on a flat surface. An **atlas** is a collection of maps. The atlas may include different types of maps: physical, political, route, and thematic. Physical maps display topographical features (mountains, rivers, and valleys). Political maps depict political boundaries (e.g., cities, states, and countries), but may also include topographical and route features. Route maps indicate roads, railways, bridges, and so forth. Thematic maps illustrate some specific data, such as land use, population, flora and fauna of an area, or literary places. Some atlases are universal in coverage while others are limited to a single country or region.

Gazetteers are geographical dictionaries that provide the location of a city, river, mountain, or other physical feature. Entries include the place name and may provide information about the population and economic characteristics of the area.

In selecting atlases, the reputation of the publisher is an important factor in determining ongoing quality. According to William A. Katz, "In the United States, the leading publishers are Rand McNally & Company, C. S. Hammond & Company, and the National Geographic Society" (Katz, 1997:68). To test the index of an atlas Katz suggests that you

> Try to find four or five names listed in the index on the maps. How long did it take, and how difficult was the task? Reverse this test by finding names on the maps and trying to locate them in the index. Difficulty at either test spells trouble. (Katz, 1997:370).

CRITERIA

In addition to the general questions identified at the beginning of this chapter, ask yourself these questions:

- Which kinds of maps are included?
- Does the atlas cover the world, a continent, a country, or a state?
- Does it include a gazetteer?
- Is statistical information included?
- If it is a historical atlas, what period of time does it cover?

Bibliographies

Bibliographies are lists of books or other forms of information. The lists identify the existence of the information, state where the information is located, or recommend items. The latter (selection tools) were discussed in Chapter 3.

The terms **trade bibliography** and **national bibliography** are used interchangeably by some authors. *Children's Books in Print* is an example of a trade bibliography. School library media specialists use it to learn if a title exists. This is an example of a source for which the compiler obtains the information from another source. In this case book publishers provide the compiler with the information about the titles they publish. This information usually includes author, title, subtitle, illustrator, publisher, and date of publication. The compiler does not examine the titles. The list merely indicates availability of a title; it is not a recommendation.

Subject bibliographies are lists limited to a specific topic and may be limited to a specific grade or age group. Many of the resources identified at the end of each chapter in this book are bibliographies designed to help you locate examples of the type of literature discussed in that chapter. Titles for subject bibliographies frequently provide information about the subject and audience of that work.

CRITERIA

In addition to the general criteria identified earlier, ask yourself these questions:

- If the bibliography lists titles for all ages, does it cover sufficient works for use in an elementary school to merit its purchase?
- Are out-of-print materials included?
- Does the compiler examine how and why items were selected for entry?
- Are the standard elements of a bibliography entry included for each item?
- Are the annotations and abstracts informative and clearly written?

Dictionaries

Dictionaries for elementary school children are usually lists of words arranged alphabetically with an illustrative sentence and a simple definition for each entry. Primary grade children can use "picture dictionaries" with their full-color illustrations. The number of entries in elementary school dictionaries ranges from 5,000 to 35,000. The front matter should explain any abbreviations and symbols used in the dictionary.

Dictionaries for older children include many of the features of dictionaries commonly used by adults. For each entry the user may find:

1. cross-references
2. syllabification (hyphenation or word division)
3. preferred and variant spelling
4. pronunciation
5. parts of speech
6. definitions
7. origin of the word
8. synonym and antonym
9. usage
10. illustrative examples
11. pictorial illustrations

The appendices may provide supplemental information about people, places, and historical events. Other features in some dictionaries are

1. charts showing population data, weights, and measures, and signs and symbols
2. lists of countries, presidents, and colleges and universities
3. style manuals, proofreaders' marks, basic rules of grammar, and forms of address and correspondence

4. first names of men and women
5. famous quotations
6. historical documents such as the U. S. Constitution.

Other types of dictionaries are specialized language dictionaries, spelling dictionaries, synonym dictionaries, and thesauri. Subject dictionaries list the words and terms used in a specific area such as sports or film.

According to Katz,

> The reputable ones [publishers of dictionaries] include Merriam-Webster; Oxford University Press; Random House; Scott, Foresman; Doubleday; Macmillan; Simon & Schuster; and Houghton Mifflin—to name the larger-better-known publishers. Among these the clear leader is Merriam-Webster (Katz, 1998: 331).

CRITERIA

In addition to the general criteria identified at the beginning of the chapter, consider these questions:

- On what basis were the main entries selected?
- Does the dictionary include colloquial and slang words, foreign words and phrases, and abbreviations?
- Does it contain encyclopedia material?
- How does the dictionary treat spelling, pronunciation, syllabification, etymology (history of the word), definition, quotations, synonyms, antonyms, usage, and syntax?
- In the dictionaries for young children are the definitions given early in the entry?

At least one unabridged dictionary is recommended for elementary schools. The choice of other dictionaries will depend on the grade levels the collection serves.

Biographical Sources

The range of biographical information can range from brief facts to extensive narratives. General biographical dictionaries provide directory-type information for people from all countries and all historical periods. As with other reference books, publishers are important. According to Katz:

> Five publishers are responsible for a large number of available biography reference titles. . . . Gale Research Inc., The H. W. Wilson Company, St. Martin's Press, Marquis Who's Who Inc., and R. R. Bowker Company (Katz, 1998: 303).

CRITERIA

In addition to the general criteria identified at the beginning of this chapter, ask yourself the following questions:

- Who wrote the biographical entry? (the editor, the subject, or an authority in the field)
- Did the subject provide the information or is it the result of the publisher's research?
- On what basis are the biographies chosen for inclusion?
- Do entries include the living and the dead?
- Is the coverage universal, national, or limited in scope?
- Is the coverage limited to people in one profession or type of work?
- Is it selective or comprehensive?
- Is it current or retrospective?
- Are the entries descriptive or critical?
- Is the information presented in the form of a narrative, an outline, or as isolated facts?

Directories

Directories provide lists of persons and organizations. Typically entries include addresses, names of key individuals, telephone and fax numbers, zip codes, e-mail addresses, Web sites, and purpose of the group. Directories may be limited to one or more organizations, government bodies, or municipalities. The scope is usually indicated in the title, such as that of a city directory. The telephone book is a directory with which children are familiar.

Other sources for directory information include encyclopedias, gazetteers, guidebooks, atlases, and government publications.

Encyclopedias

An **encyclopedia** provides information either from all branches of knowledge or from a single subject area. It is usually arranged in alphabetical order for easy access to the information. Encyclopedia sets may consist of multiple or single volumes and are organized for specific audiences. Some children's encyclopedias are designed so the beginning of the article presents basic facts and as one reads farther in the article the information becomes more complex.

When you see the phrase "continuous revision," you might wrongly assume that the articles in the encyclopedia have been completely rewritten since the previous edition. To get some clues, look on the verso of the title page for the date of the latest printing. Even this information will not tell when and how much of the encyclopedia was revised. Katz states that "Most large publishers claim to revise about 5 to 10 percent of the material each year" (Katz, 1998: 204). This is one reason schools do not purchase any one encyclopedia set on an annual basis. A common practice is to rotate the purchase of different sets over a period of three to five years. In other words, replace a specific encyclopedia every five years. Encyclopedia yearbooks, which present a summary of the year's major events, serve as supplements to the sets.

Books with the word "encyclopedia" in their title may meet different expectations. For example, *The Dorling Kindersley Visual Encyclopedia* presents facts and figures in an entertaining way that a visually oriented learner will find useful. A student trying to answer a research question may benefit from an encyclopedia that provides more in-depth coverage.

As you evaluate encyclopedias consider the following questions in addition to those identified at the beginning of this chapter:

- If the encyclopedia is for young children, are all entries beginning with the same letter in the same volume?
- Do cross-references, indexes, tables of contents, and boxed summaries help reader find related information, whether it is in the text, map, or other illustrative material?
- Do bibliographies at the end of articles lead students to further resources?
- Is there a yearbook to bring articles up-to-date?

Government Documents

The term **government document** refers to any work published by the authority of a governmental body. At the federal level the issuing agencies include the congressional, the judiciary, and the executive branches, and their departments and agencies. The documents include public records, statistical and other reports, and popular information. One example is the *United States Government Manual*, which covers organizational structure, chief officers of all government agencies, and directory type information. It is wise to keep more than one edition, as every agency may not appear in all editions.

Handbooks

Handbooks are designed to present facts about a specific topic. They should be arranged for ease of use. Some handbooks are illustrated. There are handbooks about a wide range of topics including famous facts, sports trivia, natural science field guides, and books on etiquette.

Indexes

Indexes are basic tools for retrieving information. They may be guides to locating periodical articles, poems, quotations, or book reviews. The usefulness of such indexes is dependent upon the collection's owning the journals and books indexed by these tools.

Another type of index commonly found in elementary school library collections is books of quotations or indexes to who said what and where to find it. The where, or source, is important to know if the user wants to know the context of the remark.

CRITERIA

In addition to the questions raised at the beginning of this chapter, ask yourself the following questions:

- How many of the sources of those items are owned in the collection?
- How many of the indexed items are available from nearby institutions?
- Does the index cover all items in the source?
- Does the index cover sources not found in other reference books?

Statistics

Statistical reference books are collections of numerical facts or data that have been collected and classified. In some reference sources the statistics are analyzed and interpreted. The information answers the questions of "How many?" or "How much?" A basic source for the United States is the *Statistical Abstract of the United States*. A companion work is *Historical Statistics of the United States*. These works cover a wide range of subjects including demographics, wages, production, and agriculture. When studying a historical period, students can compare the average salary, cost of living, and price of everyday items, such as a pair of shoes.

SUMMARY

Reference books are used to answer three levels of questions: ready reference, search, and research. With this in mind, one can judge how well each title provides access to information and if the appropriate type and amount of information is provided.

REFERENCES

Crosson, Vicky L. "Hey! Kids Are Patrons, Too!" *Texas Libraries* 52, no. 2 (Summer 1991): 48–50.

Katz, William A. 1997. *Introduction to Reference Work. Volume I: Basic Information Sources*. 7th ed. New York: McGraw-Hill.

Kister, Kenneth F. 1992. *Kister's Best Dictionaries for Adults and Young People: A Comparative Guide.* Phoenix, Ariz.: Oryx.

Nichols, Margaret. 1992. *Guide to Reference Books for School Media Centers.* 4th ed. Englewood, Colo.: Libraries Unlimited.

Nichols, Margaret Irby. 1986. *Selecting and Using a Core-Reference Collection.* Austin, Tex.: Texas State Library, Library Development Division.

Peterson, Carolyn Sue, and Ann D. Fenton. 1992. *Reference Books for Children.* 4th ed. Metuchen, N.J.: Scarecrow.

RECOMMENDED PROFESSIONAL RESOURCES

Booklist Includes Reference Book Bulletin. American Library Association, 1905–. Semimonthly.

The *Reference Book Bulletin* section includes reviews.

Rollins, Deborah, and Dona Helmer. 1996. *Reference Sources for Children's and Young Adult Literature.* Chicago: Booklist.

Describes over 150 titles including topical bibliographies, biographical sources about authors and illustrators, literary awards, reviews, and criticisms.

School Library Journal: The Magazine of Children's, Young Adult, and School Librarians. Cahners, 1954–.

Reference Books column in Book Review Section for February, May, August, and November issues.

Wynar, Bohdan. 1996. *Recommended Reference Books for Small and Medium-Sized Libraries and Media Centers 1996.* Englewood, Colo: Libraries Unlimited.

Recommends titles for school, public, academic, and special libraries.

REPRESENTATIVE TITLES

Abridged Readers' Guide to Periodical Literature, Author and Subject Index to a Selected List of Periodicals. Wilson, 1935–.

Bartlett's Familiar Quotations: A Collection of Passages, Phrases and Proverbs Traced to Sources in Ancient and Modern Literature. 16th ed. (Little, Brown, 1992). First published in 1855, Bartlett's is updated every ten to twelve years.

Chase's Annual Events: Special Days, Weeks & Months. Chicago: Contemporary Books, 1958–. Annual.

Identifies some 9,000 events and provides addresses for their sponsors.

Children's Books in Print. R.R. Bowker, 1969–.

An annual trade bibliography with entry by author, title, series, and illustrator.

Children's Catalog. 17th ed. (H. W. Wilson, 1996).

Includes four supplements. A standard selection tool with an analytical section useful in locating sections of anthologies and identifying books on curriculum-related topics.

Children's Magazine Guide: Subject Index to Children's Magazines. Bowker, 1948–.

A guide to journal articles designed for children in the third grade or higher. Also useful for teachers and other adults working with children to find poems, activities, and short stories on a wide range of topics related to the curriculum and to children's interests.

Current Biography Yearbook. H. W. Wilson, 1967–.

Annual cumulative collection of biographical essays that previously appeared in monthly periodical format (*Current Biography*) during the year.

The Dorling Kindersley Visual Encyclopedia, edited by Anna Kruger and others (Dorling Kindersley, 1995).

Elementary School Library Collection: A Guide to Books and Other Media Phases 1–2–3, edited by Linda L. Homa. 21st rev. ed. (Brodart Company, 1998).

A basic selection tool useful for identifying a wide range of media for use in the curriculum and to meet the reading level of students.

Famous First Facts by Joseph N. Kane. 5th ed. (H. W. Wilson, 1997).

Arranged by broad subject area. Events are indexed by the day of the month, plus year by year.

Guinness Book of World Records. Facts on File, 1955–.

A popular general information handbook, which is issued annually. Some libraries keep the most recent edition in the reference collection and circulate the older editions.

Historical Statistics of the United States. Government Printing Office, 1975 and 1979, 2 vols.

Index to Fairy Tales, 1987–1992; including 310 Collection of Fairy Tales, Folktales, Myths, and Legends: With Significant pre-1987 Titles Not Previously Indexed, compiled by Joseph W. Sprug (Scarecrow, 1944).

Index to Poetry for Children and Young People, 1993–1997: A Title, Subject, Author, and First Line Index to Poetry in Collections for Children and Young People, compiled by G. Meredith Blackburn III. (H. W. Wilson, 1998).

Handy for identifying poems related to instructional topics.

Information Please Almanac by Borgna Brunner (Houghton Mifflin, 1997).

Some reviewers rate this as more readable than *The World Almanac* and recommend it for younger readers. There are enough differences between the two books to merit having a copy of each in the collection.

Macmillan Dictionary for Children, edited by Robert Costello (Simon & Schuster, 1997).

Recommended for second graders and up.

Macmillan First Dictionary, edited by Judith Levey. Rev. ed. (Simon & Schuster's Children's, 1990).

Recommended for children as young as kindergartners.

Merriam-Webster's New Biographical Dictionary (Merriam-Webster, 1995).

Rand McNally Goode's World Atlas. (Rand McNally). Revised annually. Designed for elementary school children and is easy to use. Has close to 400 maps and approximately 36,000 entries in its index.

Science Dictionary by Seymour Simon (HarperCollins, 1994).
Clear explanations by the prolific science writer.
Something about the Author. Gale Research, 1971–.
Statistical Abstract of the United States. Government Printing Office, 1879–. Annual.
United States Government Manual. Washington, DC: Government Printing Office, 1935–.
Webster's Intermediate Dictionary (Merriam, 1994). Recommended for fourth through sixth graders.
The World Almanac and Book of Facts, 1998 edited by Robert Famighetti (World Almanac Books, 1997).
Because of the differences in coverage this makes a useful companion to *Information Please*. Both provide maps.
World Book Dictionary, edited by Robert K. Barnhart (World Book, 1998).
This unabridged dictionary is designed for children. Has clear definitions and illustrations, which help make the information accessible to children.
The World Book Encyclopedia. World Book, 1931–.
Easier ideas and concepts appear at the beginning of the longer articles, which then address more difficult coverage. Has an extensive number of cross-references, so information can be located without using the index, which is in the final volume. Numerous illustrations take up one-third of the total space of the encyclopedia.

Chapter 13

Selecting Professional Books

A professional collection offers teachers convenient access to print and nonprint materials which provide information and ideas for carrying out classroom lessons and activities. At the same time, the professional collection can also support and enrich the intellectual growth of educators as they update their knowledge.

—Pauline Potter Wilson,
*The Professional Collection
for Elementary Educators.*

EXAMINING PROFESSIONAL BOOKS

The **professional collection** is designed for a wide range of individuals who have responsibilities in the school. They include teachers, administrators, guidance counselors, social workers, nurses, speech therapists, aides, secretaries, technical staff, and others. Parents, volunteers, and other community members also may use this collection.

The collection supports an equally wide range of activities, such as

- developing curriculum and instructional units.
- identifying resources to use in teaching.
- learning more about a topic of interest.
- keeping up-to-date on educational trends and developments.

- obtaining information about teaching and learning styles.
- reading about new theories and practices.
- preparing for accreditation visits.
- keeping up-to-date on the use of technology in education.
- obtaining creative ideas for engaging children in learning.
- preparing assignments and presentations for workshops, institutes, and graduate courses.
- preparing presentations for conferences.
- conducting research.
- preparing presentations for civic and community groups.
- collecting information about educational issues for a speech.
- locating materials, guidelines, and practical tips for interns, student teachers, and new teachers.
- gathering statistical information for a report.

If there is a district level professional collection, that may be the location for research studies, statistical reports, and the archives of the school district. If no district level collection exists then these documents will be needed at the building level. In a limited number of cases, such as state standards, duplicate copies will be needed for each site.

The range of topics covered will be as broad as the interests and responsibilities of the school personnel. Some topics will be of interest to a broad range of individuals, while other topics will be primarily of interest to the individual responsible for teaching a specific subject or in charge of a specific service.

The professional collection can be used to keep personnel aware of national and state documents pertaining to education. In the 1990s a number of associations produced new guidelines and standards; these should be included. Many of the professional associations have publications about their associations and about educational issues that will be of interest to those using the collection. A sampling of the range of titles will be identified in the following section of this chapter. These suggestions are in addition to those mentioned throughout this book in the Professional Resources listings at the end of each chapter.

SPECIAL CRITERIA FOR PROFESSIONAL BOOKS

The criteria used to evaluate books for the professional collection are the same as used for all books with particular attention to:

Authority of Content

- Is the author qualified to write about this subject?
- Has the author successfully written similar works?

Appropriateness

- Does the book address the concerns of the teachers?
- Are the suggested activities appropriate for the age group served by the school?

Scope

- What is the purpose of the book?
- Does the purpose meet a known need?
- How well does the author fulfill that purpose?
- Does the author state the limitations of the book?

Accuracy

- Does the author credit the source of photographs?
- Is there an author's note?
- Does it identify the sources of information used to write the book?
- Is the information up-to-date?

Treatment

- Does the author distinguish opinions from facts?
- Does the author present unbiased opinions?
- Is there an acknowledgment section crediting content consultants?
- Does the author avoid stereotypes about race, sex, and age?
- Does the book reflect our multicultural society?

Organization of Information

- Does the information flow from one section to another?
- Does the author develop the content logically?
- Can chapters or sections of a book be used independently or must they be read in sequence?
- Does the author emphasize important ideas?
- Is there a summary or review of the major points?

Literary Merit

- Is the author's respect for and knowledge of the subject evident in the writing?
- What is your impression of the total effect of the book?

Lack of Books on the Subject

- Is there a need for a book on this subject?
- Has someone requested a book on this subject?
- Was the request based on an ongoing need or just something needed at a specific time? If people request books to do assignments in classes in which they are enrolled, they may not need the title later.

Reputation of Publisher

- Has the publisher displayed a commitment to quality books on this subject?
- Have other books by this publisher satisfied the needs of their readers?

Special Features

- What unique features does this book offer?

Ease of Use

- Is this information accurately and completely indexed?
- If the information is chronologically arranged, is there a subject index to help the reader locate information on specific topics?
- If the information is alphabetically arranged, are cross-references provided so the reader knows the terms used for the subject?
- Do chapter headings help locate information?
- How does the index help the reader locate information?
- What types of entries are included?
- Given the purpose of the book, will entries for authors, titles, illustrations, illustrators, first line of a poem, or other entries be helpful? Are these entries cross-referenced in the index? (Test the index by using different terms that mean the same thing.)
- Is the bibliography annotated?

SAMPLING OF TYPES OF BOOKS

There will be a wide range of types of books in the collection. There should be locally produced publications such as curriculum guides, resource units, instructional materials, and district policies. Documents issued by state and federal agencies regarding education should be included as well. Also included should be the whole range of theoretical and practical books about subjects in the curriculum and about services offered by the school.

Standards and Guidelines

Standards and guidelines issued by professional associations and accrediting agencies are valuable resources to have in the collection. They provide information about the latest thinking in a particular field. Making teachers and administrators aware of such publications can help them to recognize the value of the media center program as it interacts with other aspects of the total educational program.

Mentioned elsewhere in this book are the standards by the National Council of Teachers of Mathematics and the National Council for the Social Studies. Other standards developed in the 1990s include the Consortium of National Arts Education Association's *National Standards for Arts Education: What Every Young American Should Know and Be Able to Do in the Arts* and the National Council of Teachers of English and International Reading Association's *Standards for the English Language Arts*

The American Association of School Librarians and the Association for Educational Communications and Technology's *Information Power: Building Partnerships for Learning* is a good example of a book you will want to share and discuss with other faculty and staff. The chapter on "Information Literacy Standards for Student Learning" would be a good talking point with teachers to determine ways to ensure that students work toward these standards.

Annuals

Two examples of annual publications are the *Educational Media and Technology Yearbook* and *School Library Media Annual*, which review the past year's events and developments, discuss major concerns and trends, identify associations, and list recommended books for the professional collection.

Directories

A comprehensive annual is the *Directory of Video, Multimedia, and Audio-visual Products*, which includes the specifications for over 2,000 items and pieces of equipment. For information about businesses and agencies involved with the production and distribution of materials for children, one can consult *Children's Media Market Place*.

Bibliographies

Numerous bibliographies are listed in the Professional Resources for a number of chapters in this book. The following bibliographies cover a range of genres: *Books to Read Aloud with Children of All Ages*; Judy Freeman's *More Books Kids Will Sit Still For: A Read-Aloud Guide*; and Matt Berman's *What Else Should I Read? Guiding Kids to Good Books, Vol. I*. Other bibliographies cover different formats; for example, the Educators Progress Service offers a series on free materials, including *Elementary Teacher's Guide to Free Curriculum Materials*.

Instructional Technology

Established works in the area of the instructional application of technology include Robert Heinich, Michael Molenda, and Jane Russell's *Instructional Media and the New Technologies of Instruction* and Jerrold Kemp and Don Smellie's *Planning, Producing and Using Learning Technologies*.

Copyright

Teachers often have questions relating to the copyright law. A handy title is *A Copyright Primer for Educational and Industrial Media Producers* by Esther R. Sinofsky.

Reviewing Sources

As was mentioned in the chapter about selection guides, *The Elementary School Library Collection* has a section on professional materials. An entire book devoted to recommendations for professional materials is *The Professional Collection for Elementary Educators* by Patricia Potter Wilson.

Reviews about current titles can be found in standard reviewing sources, such as *School Library Journal* and *Booklist: Includes Reference Books Bulletin*. Journals published by professional associations often include reviews. Examples are the National Council of Teachers of Mathematics' *Teaching Children Mathematics* and the Association for Childhood Education International's *Childhood Education: Infancy through Early Adolescence*.

SUMMARY

The professional collection includes books on a wide range of subjects of interest to the school's personnel. As with other books in the collection, one needs to apply criteria carefully to make wise selection decisions.

TITLES MENTIONED IN THIS CHAPTER, PLUS ADDITIONAL STANDARDS

Assessment Standards for School Mathematics by the National Council of Teachers of Mathematics. National Council of Teachers of Mathematics, 1995.

Booklist: Includes Reference Books Bulletin. American Library Association, 1905–

Books to Read Aloud with Children of All Ages. Child Study Children's Books Committee. (Child Study Children's Book Committee, Bank Street College, 610 West 112th Street, New York, NY 10025; for information call 212/875–4540.)

Provides annotations for almost 400 titles, including fiction and nonfiction, to use with preschoolers through eighth graders.

Children's Media Market Place edited by Barbara Stein and Lucia Hansen. 4th ed. New York: Neal-Schuman, 1995.

Provides names, address, and ready-reference information about publishers, producers, distributors, wholesalers, and other institutions related to the production and distribution of media for children.

A Copyright Primer for Educational and Industrial Media Producers by Esther R. Sinofsky. 2nd ed. Association for Educational Communications and Technology, 1994. A comprehensive work about copyright law's implications for educators.

Curriculum and Evaluation Standards for School Mathematics by the National Council of Teachers of Mathematics. National Council of Teachers of Mathematics, 1989.

Curriculum Standards for the Social Studies by the National Council for the Social Studies. The National Council for the Social Studies, 1994. Bulletin 89.

Directory of Video, Multimedia, and Audio-visual Products by the International Communications Industries Association. Annual 1996–. Overland Park, Kans.: Daniels.

Annual directory arranged by type of media, covering the specifications for over 2,000 items and pieces of equipment.

Educational Media and Technology Yearbook. Englewood, Colo.: Libraries Unlimited.

Covers important developments of the past year.

Elementary Teacher's Guide to Free Curriculum Materials, annual. Randolph, Wisc: Educators Progress Service.

Tells how to obtain and evaluate recommended free materials.

Geography for Life: National Geography Standards 1994 by National Council for Geographic Education. National Council for Geographic Education, 1994.

Information Power: Building Partnerships for Learning by the American Association of School Librarians and Association for Educational Communications and Technology. Chicago: American Library Association, 1998.

Instructional Media and the New Technologies of Instruction by Robert Heinich, Michael Molenda, and Jane Russell. 5th ed. Merrill, 1996.

A comprehensive, well-established text that describes how new technologies can be used in teaching.

More Books Kids Will Sit Still For: A Read-Aloud Guide by Judy Freeman. New Providence, N.J.: R. R. Bowker/Reed Reference, 1995.
Provides annotations for more than 1,400 titles (picture books, poetry, folklore, fiction, and nonfiction).

National Science Education Standards by National Research Council. National Academy Press, 1996.

National Standards for Arts Education: What Every Young American Should Know and Be Able to Do in the Arts by Consortium of National Arts Education Associations. Music Educators National Conference, 1994.

National Standards for Civics and Government, by Center for Civic Education. Center for Civic Education, 1994.

Planning, Producing and Using Learning Technologies by Jerrold Kemp and Don Smellie. 7th ed. HarperCollins, 1994.
Provides step-by-step guidelines for effective use of media in instruction.

Professional Standards for Teaching Mathematics by National Council of Teachers of Mathematics. National Council of Teachers of Mathematics, 1991.

School Library Media Annual. Englewood, Colo.: Libraries Unlimited.
Covers major events and trends.

Standards for the English Language Arts by National Council of Teachers of English and International Reading Association. National Council of Teachers of English, 1996.
Designed to cover the literacy education of students in K-12 in the use of print, oral, and visual language.

What Else Should I Read? Guiding Kids to Good Books, Vol. I by Matt Berman. Englewood, Colo.: Libraries Unlimited, 1995.
Guide to help teachers conduct book discussions.

REFERENCES

Texas Education Agency. Nd. *Professional Libraries—District and School Level.* Austin, Tex.: Texas Education Agency.

Wilson, Patricia Potter. 1995. *The Professional Collection for Elementary Educators.* H. W. Wilson.

RECOMMENDED PROFESSIONAL RESOURCES

Association for Childhood Education International. *Childhood Education: Infancy through Early Adolescence.* Six times a year.
Includes reviews of children's and professional books.

Elementary School Library Collection: A Guide to Books and Other Media Phases 1–2–3. Williamsport, Pa.: Brodart, 1998.
Includes recommendations for the professional collection.

International Reading Association. *The Reading Teacher*. Eight times a year with a combined December/January issue.

Reviews children's books and professional titles. Sponsors "Teacher's Choices" on best books to use with children.

National Council for the Social Studies. *Social Studies and the Young Child*. Seven issues per year.

Includes the annual "Notable Children's Trade Books in the Field of Social Studies."

National Council of Teachers of English. *Language Arts*. Bimonthly, September, November, January, March, May, and July.

Includes the annual listing of notable books and articles about children's literature.

National Council of Teachers of Mathematics. *Teaching Children Mathematics*. Monthly except June, July, and August.

Includes reviews of children's books and professional books.

National Science Teachers Association. *Science and Children*. Monthly except June, July, August; bimonthly in December/January.

Provides reviews of children's books.

Wilson, Patricia Potter. *The Professional Collection for Elementary Educators*. H. W. Wilson, 1995.

Reports on a survey about the use of professional collections and offers recommendations about such collections. Provides descriptive annotations for materials (book and nonprint) for school library media specialists and elementary teachers.

Glossary

Accuracy: correctness of the information.

Acrylic paint: water-soluble paint that dries and becomes water-resistant.

Action patterns in narratives. *See* cliff-hanger, sensationalism, suspense, fore-shadowing, and climax.

Adapter: author who modifies traditional stories to make them accessible to contemporary readers.

Alliteration: repetition of the same consonant at the beginning of words.

Almanac: annual or biennial compendium of data and statistics relating to countries, personalities, events, and subjects

Animal story: story in which animals behave like human beings, animals behave as animals but can talk, or animals behave as animals.

Animal tale: story in which animals act and talk like human beings with exaggerated human characterization in order to teach a lesson.

Animism: attribution of conscious life and spirit to natural forms, such as plants and rocks.

Anthropomorphism: assignment of human behavior or feelings to animals.

Assonance: poetic pattern in which the same vowel sound is heard within a line or within a few lines.

Atlas: bound collection of maps.

Authentic biography: biography in which author provides documentation for sources of information and limits conversations to known statements by the individuals.

Authority: qualifications of the people (author, illustrator, editor) who created the work.

Autobiography: story of a person's life that is written by that person.

Backdrop setting: place where action occurs; a backdrop setting has no role in the story.

Balance: relationship of shapes, patterns, and colors in an illustration. When they are identical on either side of a central boundary, the work is symmetrical; when the halves are not identical the work is asymmetrical.

Ballad or folk poem: a single dramatic episode. Literary ballads share the traditional ballad characteristics but the author is known.

Beast tale: story in which one character is a trickster in animal shape.

Beginning readers. *See* Easy readers.

Bibliography: list of books or other forms of information.

Bibliography, selected: bibliography that lists bibliographical information, cost, a description, an evaluation, and a recommendation for individual items.

Big book: oversize paperback book designed to use with large groups of children reading together.

Binding: cover and materials that encase the book.

Biographical dictionary: directory-type information with brief facts or extensive narratives about people.

Biography: history of a person's life written by another individual.

Blended book: information book comprised of fictional and factual writing.

Book, physical characteristics of: binding, size, weight, paper, cover, illustrations, and typography.

Book jacket: protective cover for the book.

Chapter book: book designed for six- to nine-year-olds that ranges from 45 to 100 pages. Chapter books have fewer words, a narrower focus, fewer characters, and are less complex than novels for older children.

Characters: people, animals, or inanimate objects that carry out the actions of a story.

Characterization: manner in which the author reveals the characters.

Chronological order: narrative structure in which all events are related in the order in which they occur, for example, in terms of time of day and days in the week.

Classic: book that remains a favorite for more than one generation of children.

Cliff-hanger: suspense at the end of the chapter to set the stage for the next chapter.

Climax of narrative: the moment of high interest. It may also be the crisis or the turning point for the protagonist.

Closed ending: ending in which the twists and turns of the story have been unraveled and the reader finds a satisfactory ending.

Color attributes: characteristics of color. Three attributes are hue, intensity, and value.

Complete biography: story of the subject's life from birth to death.

Composition: arrangement of the elements in an illustration.

Concept book: information book to introduce young children to shapes, colors, sizes, a class of objects, or an abstract idea

Concrete poetry: poetry in which the meaning is conveyed by the shape of the poem or where it appears.

Condescending tone: overuse of sentiment or talking down to the reader.

Compendium: brief summary of a larger work or of a field of knowledge

Conflict, Areas of: main character (protagonist) can face a conflict against self (internal conflict of feelings within the protagonist); nature (as seen in survival stories); another person (the antagonist); or society (the rules at one's school can represent society).

Connotative meanings of words: the reader's associations with the words.

Consonance: poetic pattern in which final consonant sounds are repeated.

Contemporary realism: realistic stories about people, animals, or objects set in current times or in the past (historical fiction).

Creation myths: stories people have told to explain creation.

Crossover book: book of interest to both young readers and adults.

Cycle format: characteristic of some fantasies in which one book is linked to another through characters, settings, or both.

Denotative meanings of words: explicit meanings.

Denouement: resolution of the conflict.

Diction: author's choice of words to give the flavor of the time, place, and events.

Dictionaries, Children's: form of dictionary for elementary school children that usually has lists of words arranged alphabetically with an illustrative sentence and a simple definition for each entry.

Didacticism: instruction, often in a preachy tone.

Directory: list(s) of persons and organizations

Display face: typeface used on title pages and for the chapter headings, usually larger and more decorative than the text face.

Double spread: two facing pages on which an artist may do one illustration.

Dynamic character: character who changes as a result of the impact of the events.

Easy reader: book designed for independent use by new readers ranging in length from 31 to 64 pages, often nine inches by six inches in size, with typeface larger than that found in books for more experienced readers.

Encyclopedia: collection of information either from all branches of knowledge or from a single subject area.

End rhyme: poetic form in which sounds at the end of the line of poetry agree.

Endpapers: the first and last spreads inside the front and back cover of the book.

English language import: book from another country, such as Great Britain, Canada, and Australia, written in English and then published in the United States.

Episodic structure: the conflict and resolution in each chapter is linked to that in other chapters.

Etching: print reproduced from a metal plate on which acid is used to create the lines.

Etiological animal tales. *See* Pourquoi.

Explicit theme: theme that is stated by a character or flatly stated in a sentence.

Fable: brief, didactic tale in which an animal or inanimate object speaks as a human being and represents different aspects of human nature to teach a moral or lesson.

Fairy tale: imaginary tale involving enchantment, supernatural elements, or magical powers.

Fantasy: imaginative story about people, animals, and objects in settings outside of our daily lives.

Fiction: narrative product of the writer's imagination comprising the interdependent elements of theme, plot, setting, and characters.

Fictionalized biography: story of someone's life based on careful research in which the author personalizes the subject and creates dramatic episodes through the use of imagined conversations or expression of the character's thoughts.

Figurative language: use of figures of speech to create associations and comparisons.

Flat character: character who is not fully developed such as those in picture storybooks and in morals, where the character may have only one facet or personality trait. Minor characters in novels are often flat characters.

Folk literature: stories with uncertain origins that were handed down orally from one storyteller to another.

Folklore: beliefs, customs, superstitions, tales, art, and music of earlier times.

Folktale elements: components of folktale, specifically construction (introduction); struggle (development of the story); and major climax (the conclusion).

Foreshadowing: clues to what will happen later that provide a pattern of predictability.

Form, Poetic: structure or shape of the poem.

Formula series: series in which the main character typically is flat, one-dimensional, and does not develop.

Fractured fairy tale: spoof on a classic folk or fairy tale.

Free verse: poetry that is free of meter and may lack rhyme.

Front matter: pages between the front endpapers and the first page of text, including half-title page, frontispiece, title page, dedication page, preface, and foreword.

Gazetteers: geographical dictionaries that provide the location of cities, rivers, mountains, or other physical features.

Genre: types of literature sharing common characteristics.

Gouache: opaque watercolors.

Government document: book or other work published by the authority of a governmental body

Gutter: place in a book where the left and right pages come together.

Haiku: poem that consists of 17 syllables arranged in three lines of five, seven, and five syllables.

Handbooks: books with facts about a specific topic.

Hero myths: hero's acceptance of a dangerous assignment during which the gods may assist or hinder progress.

High fantasy: subcategory of fantasy that focuses on the conflict between good and evil.

Historical fiction: realistic stories about people, animals, or objects set in the past.

Hue: the six pure colors of red, orange, yellow, green, blue, and violet.

Humorous tales: tales that revolve around a character who makes funny mistakes; also called drolls, noodleheads, sillies, and numbskulls tales.

Hyperbole: extravagant exaggeration.

Illustrated book: book with occasional illustrations serving as decoration rather than extending the text.

Implied theme: theme revealed through the characters' actions and reactions.

Index: guide to locating periodical articles, poems, quotations, and book reviews.

Information book (nonfiction): book to inform and lead the child from a fact or facts to a concept or a principle.

Integral setting: setting that plays a role in the story and may clarify conflict with or explain a character's actions.

Intensity: brightness or dullness of a color.

Interactive books: book that involves the child, for example, by asking a question or inviting a child to repeat a word or clap to the rhythm of the words.

Interactive fiction: story in which, at the end of an episode, the reader selects from several choices to determine the progress of the action.

International literature: books originally published in languages other than English or books about children in countries outside the United States that are then published in the United States.

ISBN: International Standard Book Number.

Jobber: company that sells books from many publishers.

Leading: the space between lines of type.

Legend[1]: explanation accompanying photographs or other illustrative material.

Legend[2]: tale told as if fact about a specific historical event, person, or place.

Limerick: light verse, often nonsensical, about people's actions, manners, and idiosyncrasies. Limericks have a set rhyme scheme (a,a, b,b, a), and the third and fourth lines are shorter than the others.

Line: technique that defines objects and gives substance, shape, and mass to an illustration.

Linoleum block print: cut surface inked and pressed against paper to create a reversed impression of a design or image.

Literary elements: elements of a narration, specifically characters, plot, setting, theme, point of view, style, and tone, which function differently in different genres.

Literary fairy tale: story written by an identified author that follows the forms and elements of the traditional fairy tale literature.

Literary merit: quality of a work based on how the author deals with the literary components of theme, plot, setting, characters, and style.

Literary series: series in which the main character is rounded and three-dimensional and develops.

Lyrical poetry: poem in which poet describes emotions and thoughts rather than telling a story.

Metaphor: implied comparison of dissimilar things without using "like" or "as." One idea or object is spoken of as if it were another idea or object.

Meter: pattern of rhythm consists of beats and stresses (or stressed and unstressed syllables), with each line made up of a set number of syllables and accents in a set pattern.

Motif: smallest part of a tale that exists independently.

Myth: story told as if factual representing beliefs about supernatural forces whose characters are the gods, goddesses, and supernatural powers.

Narrative poem: poem that relates a particular event or episode or tells a long tale.

Narrative structure: arrangement of the actions in a story: chronological order and progressive or episodical plot(s).

Nature myths: stories that explain natural phenomena such as change in seasons.

Oil paint: Mix of color pigments into an oil base.

Onomatopoeia: sound that imitates the name of an object or action or illustrates the word's meaning, such as buzz or hiss.

Open ending: conclusion that is left for the reader to determine.

Organization: arrangement of the information, for example, alphabetical, chronological, tabular, statistical, classified or by geographical location

Oversimplification: simplification that distorts the information.

Page layout: placement of type and illustrations on the page.

Paperback edition: book with a paper binding.

Partial biography: life story that focuses on one period, one event, or a characteristic of the subject.

Pastels: a soft chalky drawing material similar to charcoal.

Personification: assigning human attributes to things.

Perspective: artist's use of lines and patterns to lead the viewer's eye to what the artist wants the viewer to see.

Photoessays: information presented in a balance of text and photographs.

Pictorial elements: shape, line, edge, color, proportion, detail, and space.

Picture book: book that is usually 32 pages in length (these books may be 48 or 64 pages) consisting primarily of illustrations.

Picture storybooks: genre in which pictures and text play equal roles in telling the narrative.

Plastine: form of modeling clay that never gets hard.

Plot: series of actions (what happens in the story); the story line (the sequence of events); and how the writer presents them and resolves the conflict.

Poetry: expression of ideas and feelings using words selected for their impression of sound often arranged in rhythmic patterns.

Point of view: narrator of the story, such as first person, first-person observer, author-observer, omniscient, or a combination.

Poster paint: form of tempera.

Pourquoi tale, or etiological animal tale: tale that explains phenomena of nature using animal traits or characteristics or customs of people.

Prebound book: book with reinforced binding put on prior to the book's being sold

Printmaking: transfer of an image to another surface.

Professional collection: collection designed for teachers, administrators, and others who have a wide range of responsibilities in the school.

Progressive plot: events that move from introduction, reach a climax, and end with resolution of the conflict.

Proportions: relationship of the size of one object with another, proportions may be realistic or highly exaggerated.

Protagonist: rounded character who develops through interaction with the conflict.

Proximity: relationship of distance among various objects.

Ready reference questions: request for specific information, such as a fact.

Realistic fiction: stories about people, animals, or objects set in current times (contemporary realism) or in the past (historical fiction).

Recto: the right-hand page.

Research questions: project in which the student investigates a subject thoroughly and uses many sources.

Retellers: writers who create traditional stories in a new form.

Rhythm in illustration: movement expressed by repeating colors, shapes, lines, or texture.

Rhythm of poetry: beat or regular cadence of the poem, which may be metered or spontaneous.

Rounded character: three-dimensional character with contradictions and realistic complexities and whose traits are demonstrated in the action of the story.

Science fiction: subcategory of fantasy in which scientific laws and technological inventions have a key influence on the conflict and resolution.

Scope: range of the author's goal or purpose of the book and the breadth and depth of coverage.

Scratchboard: art form in which artist scratches with tools into the painted picture surface of a two-layer board, which results in a high contrast between the remaining and absent areas.

Search questions: questions for a short report and consulting several sources (a chapter in a book, an encyclopedia article, or short magazine article).

Selection aids. *See* Bibliography, selected.

Selection tools. *See* Bibliography, selected.

Sensational tone: writing in which writer arouses the senses unnecessarily.

Sentimentality: results of a writer's creating a tearjerker situation that plays on the reader's sentiment.

Series books: formula and literary series with one character who appears in several volumes.

Setting: time and place in which the story takes place and the descriptive details about the place of action.

Setting, functions of: 1) clarify conflict, 2) serve as antagonist in survival stories, 3) illuminate character, 4) serve as symbol, such as good or evil found in folk tales.

Shape: forms created by lines, colors, and value, shapes can be flat and two-dimensional or fully rounded and three-dimensional.

Silk screening: stencil created by blocking out parts of the silk, squeezing the ink through the open mesh of the silk onto the paper, and creating an image that is not reversed.

Simile: comparison using the words "like" or "as." Subcategory of metaphor.

Source notes: notes that give the origin of the story and describe the changes made by the adapter, reteller, or editor.

Space: extent or area in two dimensions. Empty space is called a negative area while a delineated space is called a positive area.

Special features: maps, tables, graphs, photographs, and other illustrative materials; glossaries; appendixes; indexes; bibliographies; and recommended reading lists.

Static character: character who does not change during the story.

Statistical reference books: collections of numerical facts or data that have been collected and classified.

Stereotype: character with only a few traits generally attributed to a social or racial group of people.

Stock character: character with a specific personality trait or specific role in society.

Style: the author's use of words or use of pictorial elements, composition, and medium to tell a story.

Style, devices of: imagery, figurative language, personification, simile, metaphor, and rhythm.

Subject bibliography: list of information sources about a specific topic or for a specific grade or age group.

Tall tale: highly exaggerated account of exploits.

Teleology: explanation of nature that ascribes purpose to something in the natural environment.

Tempera: colored pigment mixed with a binder and water.

Theme: main idea or the central meaning of the story.

Tone: reflection of the author's feelings about the subject, characters, and readers.

Trade bibliography: list of available resources usually for one format.

Trade edition: hardback book such as one finds for sale in bookstores.

Transitional book: book designed for children moving from being a new reader to a more experienced reader. These books have a greater number of words per line, fewer illustrations, and longer chapters than books for new readers.

Translation: book originally published in a non-English language and then translated into English.

Treatment: author's presention of the material

Trickster story: tale that features one character who is a trickster in animal shape.

Typeface: size and style of the letters and characters of the text; the typeface affects the appearance and accessibility of the book.

Unity, visual: artist's technique in which various parts of an illustration are related to each other to create an integrated whole or an author's technique in relating the various literary elements to tell a story.

Value: lightness or darkness of a color, which can be changed by adding white or black.

Variants: versions of the same story that share common elements, such as the plot or character, but may have different settings or motifs

Verso: back of a page, the left-hand page.

Watercolor: mix of a powdered color with water.

Woodblock print: impression created by cutting an image into a block, inking the surface, and pressing it against the paper. The result is reversed impression of the design or image cut into the block.

Wordless books: book in which story line is told entirely with pictures or with a minimum of words.

Index

Note: Pl. refers to plate numbers.

About the Author

Phyllis Van Orden began her professional career as an elementary school librarian. More recently she has been a library educator. Her master's degree is from the University of Michigan; her doctorate in curriculum development is from Wayne State University.

Van Orden's publications include several editions of *The Collection Program in Schools: Concepts, Practices, and Information Sources* (Libraries Unlimited). The first received the Blackwell/North American Scholarship Award from the Resources Section of Library Resources and Technical Services Division of the American Library Association. She was editor of *Elementary School Library Collection* for a number of editions. She was president of the Association for Library and Information Science Education and of the Association for Library Service for Children. Her appointments included service on both the Caldecott Award and Newbery Award committees.